WHAT PEOPLE ARE SAYING ABOUT
CAROL BURTON McLEOD AND *VIBRANT*...

If anyone has the credibility to write about vibrancy, it's Carol McLeod! Carol lives life with passion and purpose, ultimately setting her gaze on Jesus Christ. In this powerful book, Carol invites readers to join her in living the vibrant life of joy they were designed to live. Writing with characteristic wisdom and wit, Carol stirs up passion in the heart of readers to become all that God intended. Get ready. Your invitation awaits!

—*Becky Harling*
Speaker; best-selling author
How to Listen So People Will Talk

Vibrant is a powerful teaching tool to help you realize that you don't have to bow to every painful and disappointing circumstance standing on your doorstep. Carol masterfully uncovers effective, time-tested, ancient keys in God's Word that will help you stay seated in your heavenly place with Christ while walking through the valley of trouble and pain. She will teach you how to be draped in God's glory even while saturated in sorrow and suffering. Born out of her own life experiences, coupled with her deep love of Scriptures, *Vibrant* is sure to propel you further into the arms of your heavenly Father when times of personal crushing and perplexities threaten to overtake you. Carol teaches that miracles of the heart happen when we tap in to the atmosphere of heaven, lifting us out of our earth-tethered mindset. This is a must read for anyone ready to mine for the gold of Holy Spirit living in the face of suffering. As a child of God, the dynamic power of the Holy Spirit is explained so beautifully through Carol's writings.

—*Christy Christopher*
Author and speaker
Incredible Intervention; Until the Day Breaks and the Shadows Flee

Just when I think, *How could Carol McLeod top the last book?* she does it again. She clearly answers the question, "How do I become the *me* who God wants me to be?" Carol is a woman who *is* becoming who God wants her to be. She speaks from her own journey—so much so that when I read the words, I hear her speaking them. This book just may be her best and most personal to date.

—*Johnie Hampton*
CEO, Hampton Creative Inc.

To increase your faith, you have to read and hear the Word of God. To speak rightly, you have to read and listen rightly. We must listen to teachers whose doctrine is sound and mirrors the Word of God—God's words in writing. In Carol McLeod's new book, *Vibrant*, well-grounded teaching will help you take a huge step up in your faith and passion for God. I explicitly trust this woman of God's instruction, encouragement, and exhortations.

—*Tim Cameron*
Author, educator, intercessor

I've always wanted to be a contagious Christian. Now I know how. Thank you, Carol McLeod, for your book, *Vibrant*. In this transformative book, you'll discover how you can be bright and striking, full of enthusiasm and energy—different. Isn't that what being a light is supposed to be? One of the highest compliments is for others to realize you're different. Reading this book will bring a fresh vision of how to let God shine through your life.

—*John Mason*
Best-selling author, *An Enemy Called Average*

Do you have trouble finding joy in every day? Are you ready to fulfill your purpose without the chains of the past holding you back? Using God's Word as the basis, Carol McLeod teaches us to walk closer to Jesus and provides the spiritual lessons we need to become vibrant women of God. I highly recommend *Vibrant* for women who want to flourish in any season of life.

—*Michelle Cox*
Best-selling author, *When God Calls the Heart* series

Do you long to live well, to feel fully alive? In *Vibrant*, Carol McLeod offers rich, spiritual truth bathed in unparalleled wisdom. This is so much more than a path to joy; it is an interactive guide to a life of purpose.

—*Angela Donadio*
Author, *Finding Joy When Life Is Out of Focus*

Carol McLeod has done it again! A must read for every woman who longs for more luster in her life. Carol provides practical advice, unlimited hope, and a proven blueprint for a vibrant life! Unpacking the promises of Scripture along with her own personal stories to keep you smiling, Carol walks with you to new places of promise.

—*Erica Wiggenhorn*
Bible teacher and author
Unexplainable Jesus: Rediscovering the God You Thought You Knew

Carol McLeod has done it again! In her latest book, *Vibrant*, she takes us on a quest to find that thing our souls thirst for. She makes us consider the origins of our perceptions, shakes up our beliefs, and guides us to a place of deeper fulfillment. You will want to make sure you have a highlighter in hand as you read this book because there are gems, nuggets, and treasure on every page. *Vibrant* provides a message you will want to read more than once—because who doesn't want to feel more alive?

—*Anita Agers-Brooks*
International speaker, life coach, and award-winning author
Getting Through What You Can't Get Over

Carol McLeod is a prolific author, inspirational speaker, and a person of deep insights. Her latest book *Vibrant* provides wonderful keys into unlocking all the special gifts God has created in you, so that you will flourish and be a vibrant reflection of His joy, freedom, and purpose for your life.

—*Amick Byram*
Actor, recording artist, and Grammy nominee

Carol McLeod is a passionate woman of God. She follows His lead in her writing and her everyday life. A gifted speaker, teacher, and writer, Carol pours her heart into all that her Savior asks her to do. It's an honor to call her my friend and a blessing to benefit from her divine-inspired wisdom with each new book she writes.

—*Lynette Eason*
Best-selling, award-winning author, *Danger Never Sleeps* series

Author Carol McLeod has given readers a great gift with her latest book, *Vibrant: Developing a Deep and Abiding Joy for All Seasons*. Not only is she presenting us with the tools to find joy, she's also providing a roadmap. Her heartfelt stories and wisdom as she applies God's word are priceless. This will be a book I return to again and again.

—*Edie Melson*
Director, Blue Ridge Mountains Christian Writers Conference

Do you want to live strong and bright in a world all too often full of pain and darkness? This kind of vibrant life is possible and author Carol McLeod shows us how in her wonderful new book, *Vibrant*. I've always appreciated McLeod's brilliance in helping her readers understand where Scripture and real life intersect. Not only does *Vibrant* instruct, but it also inspires growth as we trust God for all things, encouraged by truths such as this: "When God the Father first thought of you, He thought of a person who would be filled with His very own character. It was His holy and high intention that you would live a life not scarred by pain but made beautiful by pain. He needed a vessel just like you that would partner with Him in splashing His joy, hope, and life all over this crazy and dark world in which we live." For anyone longing for more purpose, power, and peace, this book will most certainly accelerate your growth!

—*Lucinda Secrest McDowell*
Author, *Soul Strong* and *Life-Giving Choices*

Vibrant

Developing a Deep and Abiding
Joy for All Seasons

CAROL McLEOD

WHITAKER
HOUSE

VIBRANT
Developing a Deep and Abiding Joy for All Seasons

Carol Burton McLeod
carol@carolmcleodministries.com
www.carolmcleodministries.com
Carol McLeod Ministries
P.O. Box 1274
Orchard Park, NY 14127
855-569-5433

ISBN: 978-1-64123-495-5
eBook ISBN: 978-1-64123-496-2
Printed in the United States of America

© 2020 by Carol Burton McLeod

Whitaker House
1030 Hunt Valley Circle
New Kensington, PA 15068
www.whitakerhouse.com

Library of Congress Control Number: 2020945638

Dedication

Lovingly dedicated to the best friends a girl could ever have.

Shannon Maitre

Although we are not sisters by blood, we are certainly sisters by divine intervention! How I have loved mentoring you over the years—and now you mentor me! I love watching you love others, dig for gold in Scripture, and share your own unique brand of joy on the world. You, dear one, are a treasure.

And when we both get older
With walking canes and hair of gray
Have no fear even though it's hard to hear
I will stand here close and say,
Thank you for being a friend[1]

Dawn Frink

Oh! What a wise and wonderful gift you have been to me! You have loved me when I wasn't very lovable and have weathered many storms with me. You are a woman of substance and value. I would rather go for a walk with you, drink tea with you, and absorb your grace than any other woman I know.

Winter, spring, summer or fall
All you have to do is call
And I'll be there, yes, I will
You've got a friend[2]

1. Andrew Gold, "Thank You for Being a Friend," on *All This and Heaven Too* (Asylum Records, 1978).
2. Carole King, "You've Got a Friend," on *Tapestry* (Ode Records, 1971).

Contents

Part Three: The Secret Garden of the Soul

Part Four: "Whatever!"

Part Five: Walk Worthy

Part Six: It's Enough

Part Seven: Being Not Doing

Part Eight: One Final Invitation

Foreword

About ten years ago, I was filming a scene for a movie on a magnificent hillside in Italy. It was 3 a.m., we'd been working for forty-eight hours straight ... and it was raining. It was the kind of hard, freezing rain that goes deep into your bones and starts to paralyze you. I was tired, frustrated, soaking wet, and cold.

And yet *I was having the time of my life.* As I stood there, absolutely miserable on the outside, I realized that this was what I was born to do. As a result, I was more than happy—I was *vibrant.*

Honestly, there have been numerous moments like that one throughout my life. In many ways, they were moments of revelation, because in spite of the difficult circumstances, I discovered I was loving every minute, no matter what the challenge.

The truth is, I always look at a glass as half-full rather than half-empty. Since I was evidently born to see the positive side in just about everything, I can't take the credit. But that ability has had a profound impact on my life and career. That's not to say I haven't experienced tough times, but I've discovered that how you respond to those difficulties is far more important than the difficulties themselves.

My job as a filmmaker and media coach is to help people share their story with the largest possible audience. After all, everyone has a story, but in today's media-saturated, distracted, and disconnected world, most of those people struggle to get their voices heard. My particular focus is the intersection of faith, media, and culture, so I spend a great deal of time writing books and speaking at events filled with people who are eager to tell stories about their own faith experience.

And keep in mind that in spite of all the media opportunities out there today, it's that very flood of media clutter that makes it more difficult than ever to connect. In fact, some research suggests that we're so distracted and have so many options that when we meet someone for the first time, we decide what we think about that person within the first four to eight seconds.

Think about that for a minute. You haven't had time to get to know the person or listen to what they have to say. But in a world where we're being bombarded with as many as 10,000 media messages every single day, we have plenty of other options. So we've actually changed our behavior to the point where we start making decisions about things before we even have the chance to fully experience them.

Needless to say, it's a recipe for a culture of isolation.

For instance, when co-writer Jonathan Bock and I were researching our book *The Way Back: How Christians Blew Our Credibility and How We Get It Back*, we discovered a fascinating fact: 69 percent of Americans don't know their neighbor's name! That means more than two-thirds of our population doesn't know the person living next door, across the street, or down the hall. Certainly there are many things to blame—social media, mobile phones, digital distractions—but the implication is staggering for our culture, our communities, and our relationships.

It's also a growing global crisis, and a big part of the reason the United Kingdom recently designated a minister for loneliness in the prime minister's cabinet. A press release announcing the position explained, "Three quarters of general practitioners surveyed have said they are seeing between one and five people a day suffering with loneliness, which is linked to a range of damaging health impacts, like heart disease, strokes and Alzheimer's disease. Around 200,000 older people have not had a conversation with a friend or relative in more than a month."

Clearly, there's a crisis of loneliness in our world today.

But one thing I've learned over the years is that joy dissolves the isolation. Like a magnet, people are drawn to joyful and vibrant people like moths to a flame, without that nasty problem of being burned in the process.

The bottom line is that whatever your message, calling, or passion, if you want to impact other people, becoming more vibrant and joyful is the single most important way to capture their attention.

Because of my career, I'm on a plane just about every week. Early one morning, I boarded a flight and was upgraded to first class. I sat next to a very nice elderly woman who was obviously not terribly familiar with flying. She struggled with her seatbelt for a minute or two before I reached over and fixed the problem. In the process, I made a joke about it.

Surprised, she said quite loudly, "How can you make a joke this early in the morning? It's way too early to be happy!" We both laughed, and it started a conversation that allowed me to share where my joy comes from, which naturally led to a discussion about my Christian faith.

Whatever your idea, message, passion, or gift, you're about to learn how living a vibrant life will open doors you never dreamed you could open. I've known Carol McLeod for decades, and I'm convinced you're in remarkable hands. Honestly, I've never seen another book quite like this, and when I read the manuscript, I knew it would be a game changer for millions of people.

Perhaps you've spent your life seeing the glass as half-empty. Perhaps you've never known how to express the kind of vibrant life this book is about. Or perhaps you've experienced great tragedy, abuse, or neglect, and can't imagine another option.

Whatever your background and whatever you've experienced, I can guarantee your story isn't over. Just as I realized on that freezing cold and wet Italian hillside many years ago, when you discover what you're born to do, it will change everything.

—*Phil Cooke, Phd.D.*
Founder/CEO, Cooke Media Group
Author, *Maximize Your Influence: How to Make Digital Media Work for Your Church, Your Ministry, and You*

Acknowledgments

My life has been a vibrant display of people, events, and history that has created the glorious garden in which I find myself standing today. It's a delight for me to just take a moment and breathe in the fragrances of relationships that have been gifted to me over the years.

Craig: I always tell young women that other than accepting Jesus as their Lord and Savior, who they choose to marry is the most monumental decision of their entire lives. I am so grateful I chose you! You are kind, wise, supportive, and godly in all your ways. What a gift you have been to me!

Matthew: How I love seeing you become the man you were created to be from the beginning of time! I always knew that you were bound for greatness and so I am not surprised by the life that you are living. Keep believing, keep praying, and keep leading, my son. You are so loved.

Emily: You are a vibrant friend, a dedicated servant, an excellent teacher, and a faithful mom. You are tending the garden of your family so well. I admire you greatly. You are so loved.

Christopher: Your heart, your perspective, and your attitudes are a resilient demonstration of what is possible in the life of a person who simply refuses to give up. Amelia and Jack are so blessed to call you Daddy. You are doing a great job, my son. Keep going. The best is yet to come. You are so loved.

Jordan: What a grand delight it has been to watch your life and to see you grow into your calling as a husband, a father, a worship leader, and a talented producer. You have made my life so rich with your friendship and with your faith. You are so loved.

Allie: I think that your middle name just might be "Vibrant"! You make life so much more dazzling just with your very presence. I love celebrating holidays with you, praying with you, and watching you use your gifts and talents in God's kingdom. You are so loved.

Joy: How could I have known, when you were just a little girl, the treasure that you would become in these years of my life? I have loved watching you stand in unremitting faith to give birth to a family. I want to be just like you when I grow up. You are so loved.

Chris: You are the son-in-law for whom I prayed for many years. What a delight that God answered my prayers with you! Thank you for loving Joy so well and for celebrating her. Know that I believe in you, Chris, and that I am cheering for you wildly as you finish medical school. You are so loved.

Joni: I have cherished you since the day you were born. As I held you in my arms, I knew that there was a calling and purpose on your life that only God could have given to you. Know that I am praying for you and that I am always just a phone call away. I am your mom and my heart is always turned toward you. You are so loved.

Olivia Mae: Someday you will be the one writing the books in this family! Your sweet spirit and obedient heart are a delight to everyone who knows you. As you stand on the precipice of the teen years, keep choosing Jesus. He is the best choice you will ever make. You are so loved.

Ian Wesley: God is going to use you, Ian, so keep close to Him all the days of your life. Hide God's Word in your heart and honor Him in all that you do. Keep reading, keep drawing, and keep dreaming. I love cheering for the Bills and for Duke with you! You are so loved.

Wesley Eric: You are well-named, sweet boy, and have the stabilizing characteristics of the Wesleys who have gone before you. You are insightful, sensitive, and possess a servant's heart. Can't wait to watch you in the Final Four someday! You are so loved.

Amelia Grace: You lead with kindness and with friendship, my darling girl. Your quiet sparkle is a refreshing oasis in all of our lives. I miss you every single day that we are not together. "A" stands for "Amazing" and for "Amelia"! You are so loved.

Boyce: You are perceptive, extremely thankful for the life you have been given and are charged with an energy that is uncommon! Keep being the warrior that God created you to be. I love your questions, admire your tenacity, and deeply enjoy your enthusiasm. You are so loved!

Elizabeth Joy: You are a bundle of heaven-sent delight in one little girl package! You keep us laughing and filled with the promise of the future. You have captivated all of our hearts and I can't wait to see what God has for you! You are so loved!

Jack: To the boy who loves trains, robots, the solar system, and his dad! Every time I look at your face or hear your voice, I am filled to overflowing with a precious joy that is undeniable. Obey your dad and enjoy being a boy! Thanks for loving Christmas with me. I love cheering for the Bills and for UNC with you and your dad! You are so loved!

Mom and Leo: Thanks for loving me and for believing in me. My heart just aches to be with you, but know that I can always feel your prayers.

Nanny: Your example of godly living has inspired our entire family! Keep praying for all of us!

Norman Burton: My wonderful dad who now lives in eternity with Jesus. I wouldn't be the woman I am without having had you as my earthly father. All the credit goes to you, and all the glory goes to God.

The hard-working, generous and incomparable staff of Carol McLeod Ministries: Angela Storm, Linda Zielinski, Danielle Stoltz, Kirsten Monroe, Caleb Wiley, Christy Christopher, and Kim Worden. Don't we have fun together? Thanks for being my right hand, my left hand, my entire brain, and extraordinary friends. I love serving God with you.

John Mason: My friend and literary agent who has opened door after door for me! You and the Holy Spirit are a great team!

The staff at Whitaker House: Thanks for taking a chance on this persuasive, enthusiastic, and persistent author! Your friendship and your professionalism mean the world to me. I am honored and blessed to be a Whitaker House author. Bob Whitaker, Christine Whitaker, Peg Fallon, Jim Armstrong, and Becky Speer—you each have become so very dear to me.

And, of course, a special shout-out to the Carol McLeod Ministries Board of Directors! Angela Storm, Kim Pickard Dudley, Sue Hilchey, Shannon Maitre, Tim Harner, Taci Darnelle, and Suzanne Kuhn. You all are the foundation of everything that we do. Thanks for being rock solid! Thanks for fertilizing this entire operation with wisdom, expertise, and personal support.

Christy Christopher: My fearless leader in prayer. When we get to heaven, we will realize the victories that you won on my behalf. I appreciate your commitment to prayer and your friendship more than words could ever express. Thank you for not being afraid of the battle!

Warrior Moms: What an honor it has been to fight battles with you! We are standing in strong faith that with God nothing is impossible. Thank you for holding up my arms in the battle.

Thank you also to the group of women who answer the desperate e-mails that come into Carol McLeod Ministries: Linda Hoeflich, Debby Summers, Angela Storm, Carolyn Hogan, Diane Phelps, Jill Janus, Shannon Maitre, Susie Hilchey, Debby Edwards, and Christy Christopher—God is using you in mighty and dramatic ways! I am honored to partner with you in prayer and in encouragement.

And then, to a magnificent team of friends who fill my life with encouragement and joy: Carolyn Hogan, Lisa Keller, Jill Janus, Dawn Frink, Lynn Fields, Debby Edwards, Diane Phelps, Brenda Mutton, Elaine Wheatley, Becky Harling, Monica Orzechowski, Melissa Thompson, Marilynda Lynch, Joy Knox, Sue Hilchey, Kim Pickard Dudley, Shannon Maitre, and Christy Christopher. Each one of you is a priceless gift from a loving and gracious Father.

And to Jesus, my Lord and Savior! Thank You for calling me, equipping me, anointing me, and choosing me for Your grand purposes. I live to make hell smaller and heaven bigger! I live to honor You with every breath, with every word, and with every minute of my life. You have made my life vibrant beyond my wildest dreams!

Introduction

Have you ever met someone who possessed a quiet radiance so rich and so dynamic that you ached for more? This unique individual may have exuded more than just a mere sparkle but wordlessly communicated a deep and abiding joy. Have you ever met a person like that? I have and when I met her, I determined then and there that I wanted what she had. It's not that I wanted to *be* her, but I did want to be *like* her.

Perhaps you have a friend or a family member whose presence is profoundly compelling and they are able to revive the dead places in your life in just a single conversation or with a mere word of encouragement. If you know someone like this, you anticipate your times together and yearn for just one more minute of conversation.

As you observed this unique individual, you might have realized that their joy was contagious, their peace was deep, and their compassion was engaging. Sometimes, when you meet a person with those outstanding characteristics, you place them in a certain category, thinking of Mary

Poppins, Pollyanna, or even "hmm...shallow." However, if you make the effort to take a longer look at this radiant individual's life, you might just realize that their persona is not attached to their circumstances but rather to their convictions.

This person is simply *vibrant*, regardless of their socioeconomic level, education, marital status, or health. This person has determined to live their life in a manner that is both compelling and magnetic.

The ability to live a vibrant life, I believe, comes from two distinct determinates in life: first, the ability to suffer well no matter the cost to personal preference or desires; and second, an attachment to Someone greater than self. This book will present the case for both dynamic disciplines that are a prerequisite to living a vibrant life.

Vibrant is both a *how-to* book and a *what-to* book. Although you may not see lists named "How to..." or "What to...," make no mistake about it, they are on every page, between every sentence, and bursting out of every word.

What to *Be*

What is it that we are meant to *be* as believers in Jesus Christ? Is there a heavenly cookie cutter that somehow cuts us all out of the same shape so that we taste, appear, and resemble one another completely? Although I don't believe that there is a divine cookie cutter that determines your personality, I do believe that we are all made in the image of the One who created us.

What are some of the character traits and attitudes that we are called to exude as we live our life in the land of disappointment, rejection, and discouragement? Are there expected disciplines that will guarantee Christlike behavior in a world gone mad? Does the Father expect our personalities to mimic one another as we dance through this experience known as *time*? More importantly, when Christ and His divine nature come to take up residence inside of a mere mortal, what changes must be made to accommodate His amazing presence?

As I have walked with Christ for over half of a century, I have struggled with this very issue, wondering, *What must I do to become less like me and more like Him? Is there a formula? A vitamin? Is it possible to earn a degree in the character of Christ? What must I do?*

Vibrant, therefore, will also answer necessary questions like these:

+ What are some of the expected, and yet very fulfilling, behaviors expected for a believer in Jesus Christ?

+ Do I still get to be *me?*

+ Am I expected to be perfect?

+ Can I still have fun?

+ Is this just an act? Do I just read the script rather than be the real me?

+ Where is the blueprint found for this type of living?

How to...

Although I can't tell you how to lose fifty pounds and keep them off, how to bake a mouthwatering chocolate cake, or how to refurbish a 1950s car, I *can* tell you how to live for Jesus. I can instruct you how to live a life so rich and so glorious that the people in your world will ache for what you have. After years of reading and studying Scripture, and decades of living enthusiastically for Christ and His kingdom, I believe that I have the insight to teach you this miraculous way of life. I can coach you by using the Bible as our source and laying out a practical, daily strategy for living a miraculously vibrant life.

Although the process is far from easy, it is indeed simple.

Even a person who has been pummeled by the circumstances of life will be able to catch a fresh vision and learn how to flourish once again. You see, circumstances do not have the power to determine what type of life you will live. Only you and the Holy Spirit in you have that dynamic power! Disappointments, discouragement, and rejection might have distracted you but the Word of God will brilliantly redirect your heart and your choices toward Christ and His unshakable kingdom.

More often than I would have preferred, I have asked myself:

+ How do I still stay me and yet become like Him when my world has collapsed?

+ Why has this happened to me?

+ Is it possible for me to live a life of joy and purpose while living in the middle of this mess?

To help you become the *Vibrant* person you can be, we will address questions such as:

+ How do I move beyond past pain?

+ How do I remove weeds such as anger, bitterness, and impatience that have grown in my heart?

+ How do I repair the damage of the past?

+ How do I cultivate a new way of living?

+ Is there a new normal—a *better* normal? If so, what is it and where do I find it?

+ How do I become the *me* that God wants me to be?

Undeniable

We will take a long, lingering look at New Testament Scriptures that clearly invite believers of every generation to live an extraordinarily rich and vital life. There is no greater place to look for eternal truth than in the Word of God. There is no lovelier mirror to look into than the sacred pages of Scripture. There is no other call so gracious and yet so compelling as the invitation to simply become more and more like Jesus.

You see, my friend, you will never live a vibrant life on your own strength or due to your own mental calculations. You need more than what you, as a human, have to offer in order to live an undeniably passionate and luminous life.

You need Jesus, you need the power of the Holy Spirit, and you need His eternal Word. When you combine your weakness with His strength, the certain result is a miracle! When you add the wisdom of His Word to the fragility of your human thinking, you will experience the mind of Christ. When you ask the Holy Spirit to fill you with His ageless power, you will be the person who was in the Father's heart at the beginning of eternity.

For You formed my inward parts; You wove me in my mother's womb. I will give thanks to You, for I am fearfully and wonderfully made; wonderful are Your works, and my soul knows it very well. My frame was not hidden from You, when I was made in secret, and skillfully wrought in the depths of the earth; Your eyes have seen my unformed substance; and in Your book were all written the days that were ordained for me, when as yet there was not one of them. —Psalm 139:13–16

When God the Father first thought of you, He thought of a person who would be filled with His very own character. It was His holy and high intention that you would live a life not scarred by pain but made beautiful by pain. He needed a vessel just like you to partner with Him in splashing His joy, hope, and life all over this crazy and dark world in which we live. You were chosen by the One whose very name is life (see John 14:6) to live vibrantly at your moment in history. Not only have you been given the job of living vibrantly, but you have also been fully equipped to live a vibrant and expansive life.

It's Time to Explore

I'd like to invite you to join me on a grand adventure as we discover the source of life, the meaning of life, and the purpose of living well. The expedition on which we are about to embark will be challenging but fulfilling. We will view luscious and magnificent possibilities, traveling through dry and arid places to reach our intended goal. As you learn from this exciting journey, you will also be handed a treasure map of sorts that will be filled with choices. Only you can decide what direction you will take.

The interactive map will ask you questions that, again, only you can answer.

+ Is this the life you want to live?

+ What kind of person do you want to be?

+ Are you being the best *you* possible?

+ Can you be kinder? More loving? More passionate?

+ Can you show a greater grace? Can you be a better friend?

+ How have you been designed to be a vessel of joy? Of peace? Of hope?

+ Are you using your time for things that truly matter in life?

So, my friend, gear up! Set your face to the sunrise and fill your heart with unmatched possibilities. Determine this day that whatever vibrant means, *you want it!* Tell yourself and anyone who will listen, "If I am nothing else, I *will* be vibrant."

Would you pray this prayer with me today?

Lord Jesus, I want everything that You have for me. I desire to be a vibrant demonstration of Your character on earth. I pray that as You reveal Yourself to me, I will become more and more like You every day. In Jesus's name I pray. Amen.

⌒

We become what we purpose to become—what we
are intentional about becoming.
—Heidi St. John

1

But What Does It Mean to Be Vibrant?

Have you ever smugly assumed that you knew what a certain word meant, but when you looked up its definition in a dictionary, you discovered that it meant something else entirely?! Such is my relationship with the word *vibrant*.

When I was explaining to my lifelong mentor that the title of this book would be *Vibrant*, she peered at me over her bifocals with a question mark etched into her lovely yet wrinkled face and queried, "But what does vibrant mean?"

Although she has lived for over seven decades, this lady with a spring in her step is quite savvy when it comes to technology. She quickly pulled up the definition on her smartphone.

"Moving to and fro rapidly," she read to me dryly. "Oscillating or pulsating rapidly, readily set in vibration."

I looked at her as if she had lost her senses. I wondered if she had been sitting on her heating pad too long.

"That's *surely* not what it means," I emphatically replied. "At least, that's not what I *thought* it meant."

Although she was gracious enough not to say it aloud, I knew this sage woman was thinking, *Carol, if you are going to write a book about something, you better know what it means!*

And so began my journey into understanding the meaning of this elusive but powerful word.

According to Webster...and Carol

When I was in the fifth grade, Miss Sullivan lovingly called her students' dictionaries "your little red friend." We each had one on top of our desk on the first day of school and we were expected to use it often. We participated in dictionary drills and spelling bees; there was daily time set aside for reading out loud from "our little red friend." If someone in the classroom had the audacity to ask the severe Miss Sullivan what a word meant, she would slap her ruler on the guilty student's desk and command, "Get out your little red friend!"

Believe it or not, that was the year I fell in love with words. I *loved* to discover antonyms, synonyms, definitions, and word derivations. While other students were fascinated by the Beatles, Sandy Koufax, and Peggy Fleming, I was thinking about parts of speech, word usage, and alphabetical order.

It should come as no surprise, then, that when my dear mentor challenged me concerning the meaning of the word "vibrant" nearly five decades after the fifth grade, I dug ferociously for meaning and for derivation.

According to the dictionary, the word "vibrant" is an adjective and among its meanings are: "pulsating with life, vigor or activity," "oscillating or pulsating rapidly," "readily set in vibration," "responsive, sensitive," "sounding as a result of vibration : resonant," and "bright."

As I read this very official definition of my new favorite word, I realized that although it was beginning to make better sense to me, I still had some research to do in order to thoroughly understand the meaning of *vibrant*.

This word first appeared in print in 1616 and it has apparently stood the test of time … unlike other words that were birthed that same year, like *bemock* (mock) and *eleemosynary* (charitable).

As I continued through the word search that I hoped would lead me toward greater understanding, I learned that vibrant comes from the Latin *vibrare*, which means "to agitate," hence the English meaning of "pulsating with life, vigor or activity."

My treasure hunt led me to more definitions for *vibrant*—and I finally found a wordsmith's pot of gold. Under the secondary definitions for vibrant, I found this rare paragon of knowledge:

+ Having or showing great life, activity and energy

+ Very bright and strong

That's what I thought! A vibrant person shows great life, great activity, and great energy. A vibrant person is *alive* in the deepest part of his or her soul and flourishes in every season of life. A vibrant person *knows* the secret of thriving in the most adverse of conditions.

Perhaps *I* need to write a dictionary! This would be my definition of vibrant:

+ Showing life enthusiastically, a high level of inner energy

+ Flourishing in every season of life

+ The ability to thrive in the most adverse of living conditions

+ Lavish and exuberant growth that reveals itself in uncommon and captivating ways

The Sacred Invitation

I can't speak for you. I can only speak for me and for the desires that are stirring within my own heart. I want to live vibrantly with a ferocious ardor and an unremitting hunger. I want to live a life so noble and meaningful that heaven gasps in awe and in wonder. I deeply thirst for a living dynamic that smacks of eternity and causes the enemy and his obnoxious companions to cower in fear and shame.

I will embrace a vibrant existence even if no one else joins me on this thrilling journey. However, my new friend, consider yourself invited!

You, my friend,
Are cordially invited
By the Creator of the Universe and the Lover of your soul
To Live a Vibrant Life.
RSVP Daily

It is time to prepare the soil of our hearts for a vibrant crop of miraculous growth and remarkable beauty. I hope that this book will become your companion in this growing season and in many to come. God's desire is that your life becomes a well-watered demonstration of His beauty and wonder. You were created to be a vibrant show-and-tell of all that God is. Your heart, and therefore your life, was made for unseasonable abundance and for radiant delight. You, my friend, were made to be vibrant!

Would you pray with me today:

Lord Jesus, I respond to Your holy invitation to join my life with Yours in the ability to live a vibrant life. I long to thrive in the most adverse of conditions and to flourish in every season of life. I am Yours, Lord, so water me with Your word. In Jesus's name I pray. Amen.

The whole world is a series of miracles, but we're so used to them we call them ordinary things.
—Hans Christian Andersen

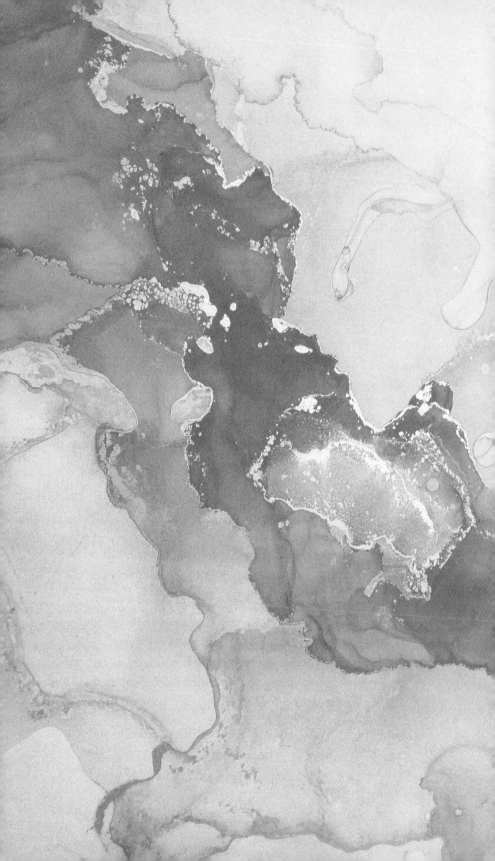

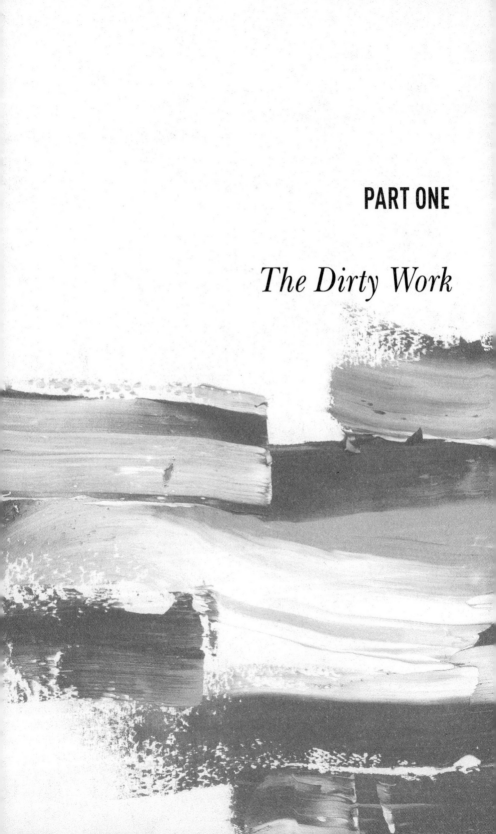

PART ONE

The Dirty Work

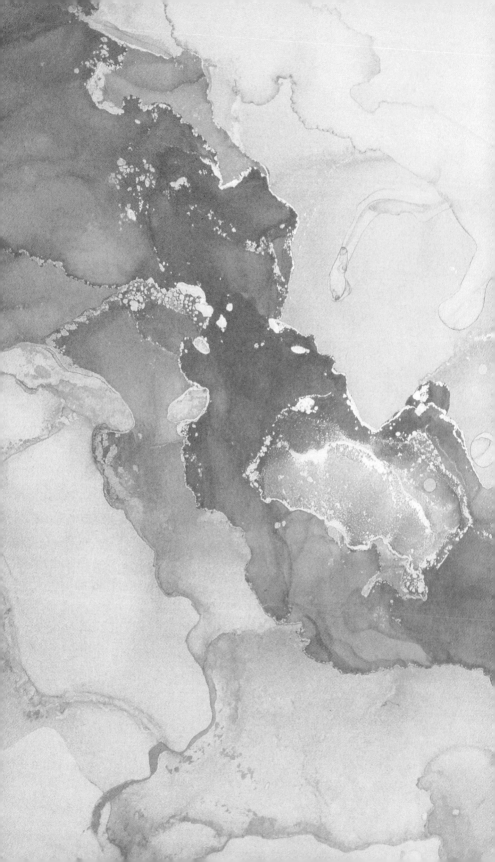

2

Dare to Prepare

After wrestling with Noah Webster and then embracing a definition of the word *vibrant* that resonated within my soul, I began to wonder about a new aspect of this lovely word, pondering, *Is there a single prerequisite that one must adhere to in order to live a vibrant life?*

As you can imagine, I came upon my answer in a roundabout manner. I decided to study horticulture in order to determine *how to cultivate vibrancy.*

Prepare the Soil

When a world-class agriculturalist prepares to plant an award-winning garden, many things must occur before even one seed is placed in the ground. The gardener begins to prepare next year's soil immediately after harvest. It takes mulching, fertilizing, and plowing; a person with a *radiant* green thumb will often add nutrients, subtract weeds, and hope for just the right amount of rain. The process of guaranteeing that a plot of dirt will develop into a vibrant garden is long, painstaking, and demanding. However, it is worth it, my friend! We are about to learn that it is oh, so worth it.

The next task in preparing the soil for an abundant harvest is to acknowledge the importance of digging deeply. A successful farmer knows the utmost importance of loosening the soil and removing any rocks or roots that may have made a home in the plot of earth that will eventually become a productive garden. This farmer is intent on digging well below the surface of the earth to ensure that the seeds he or she eventually plants will nestle down snugly into the warmth and freedom of this soil.

Digging Deeply

You, too, must dig deeply into the promises in God's Word if you hope that your life will display the abundance of the Father. You must remove the rocks of worry, discouragement, and sin. You must throw away the stones of unforgiveness, bitterness, and compromise. You will never have the sustaining ability to live a vital and dynamic life without removing the gravel of offense.

When you take the time to dig deeply into the Bible and allow it to become part of the rich soil of your life, you will be utterly surprised at what it digs up in you. I often *dare* people to do an experiment with the Word of God—a dare that I present to you today.

I dare you to read the Bible every day for twenty-one days for just ten minutes a day. Try not to miss a day, but if you do, start right up again. I believe that at the end of this three-week period, you will see a marked difference in the way that you process life as well as how you treat other people.

When you immerse yourself into the powerful truth of the Bible on a daily basis, suddenly you will realize, *I didn't lose my temper with my children this morning. What happened to me?*

The Word happened to you!

You discover, *I wasn't cranky with my mother when she called me for the tenth time today! What happened to me?!*

The Word of God happened to you!

You wonder, *What's happened to me?! I didn't even get angry when my husband forgot to take out the trash!*

The Word of God happened to you!

You feel joyful for your friend who's getting married instead of self-pity because you are not even dating anyone and you ponder, *What happened to me?!*

The Word of God happened to you!

Spending time ingesting the eternal and life-changing Word of God every day is one of the sweetest disciplines that precedes embracing a vibrant life. The call to read God's love letter and apply it personally to your life will be found often on the pages of this Book. It is impossible to overestimate the life change that will happen to you when you drink in the treasure of the most glorious and impactful Book ever written.

Just One Choice

I was recently invited to sit on a panel consisting of amazing women authors and speakers for a national women's conference. We fielded several interesting questions, such as:

- How did you get started in the publishing industry?
- What is the greatest miracle you have ever experienced in your life?
- If you could tell one thing to the twelve-year-old you, what would it be?

We were nearing the end of the panel discussion when the moderator pulled a question out of the basket, read it silently, and then smiled as she read the question for everyone to hear, "What is the one piece of advice that you would give to a person that could change his or her life forever?"

The moderator paused and said, "Carol, you answer first."

It was a good thing that she gave the nod to me because I was sitting on the edge of my seat. It was all that I could do not to wave my arms wildly in the air in order to get her attention.

I answered this difficult yet easy question in just three words: "Read your Bible."

I handed the microphone to the well-known author beside me, who said, "I agree with Carol."

The next author responded with just four words: "I can't top that."

The fourth author on the panel grinned. "Works for me!" she exclaimed.

"That's it," agreed the last speaker, a gifted author, worship leader, and Bible teacher.

And I truly meant it. *I know that I know that I know* this much: reading the Bible is the one choice of *prime importance* that a believer in Jesus Christ must make in order to live abundantly and fully.

So, as you begin the dirty work of preparing the soil of your heart to live the life that it was made for, start with digging deeply into the inspired truth that is found only in the Bible. The Word will do an excavating work in your life that will equip you to grow a world-class array of delicious fruit and gorgeous flowers. When you honor the Word of God in your life, the world will stand in awe at the life that has been grown in the dirty soil of your formerly insignificant existence.

You were created to be a producer of delectable fruit, brilliant flowers, and undeniable glory. The Word of God will prepare your life for the demonstration of God's character in an ordinary man or in a common woman.

Would you pray with me today:

Lord Jesus, prepare the soil of my heart so that I become a fruit-bearing Christian. Would You stir up the desire in me to read Your Word consistently and passionately? Thank You,

Father, for transforming my life as I read the Bible. In Jesus's name I pray. Amen.

So will My word be which goes forth from My mouth; it will not return to Me empty, without accomplishing what I desire, and without succeeding in the matter for which I sent it.

—Isaiah 55:11

Visit many good books but live in the Bible.

—C. H. Spurgeon

3

Manure Matters

Are you ready for the next step in preparing the soil of your heart for a bumper crop of the character of the Father? Aren't you excited to discover what comes next?

The second step that an award-winning gardener takes in preparing the soil for a bumper crop is that he or she will add manure to their future garden. While it is true that some agriculturalists will add chemical fertilizer, the purest, most organic manner with which to pretreat soil for rapid growth is to add manure. Gardening manuals state that the best soil has a 50/50 mix, which means 50 percent soil and 50 percent manure or compost.

Farmer's manuals may call for *dehydrated cow manure* or *well-rotted horse manure* instead of man-made fertilizers. That doesn't sound like much fun to me; does it to you? Manure smells, it's revolting to its core, and I can't even let my mind travel to the place from whence it came!

The Miracle of Manure

Have you ever had a load of manure dumped on you? I have had it happen to me many times and it is disgusting! Now, I am not talking about actual manure, of course, but times in my life when people gossiped about me, when finances failed me, and when my health was weakened. I have felt attacked by the sewage of others when I have been rejected or when my children have been mistreated. Initially, a heap of manure dumped upon someone's life is putrid and vile. However, the long-term experience of being covered in circumstantial manure is only offensive momentarily because as time does its work in the makeup of the manure, a miracle happens.

There are times in all of our lives when the hard stuff prepares us for the great stuff. There are seasons when the situation in life that stinks the most is often what will cause the most beautiful growth. It is vital to remember that it is possible to *grow through* what you *go through*.

I hope that you have come to realize that the lessons one learns from gardening can be easily applied to life. One of these lessons is that the hardest, the most difficult, and the ugliest days of life are able to create the desired environment for ravishing growth. As I look back at my life, I can assure you of the truth of that statement. I have learned to allow the difficulties in life to act as fertilizer in the garden of my soul. When life throws something vile and wasteful on me, I simply plant another crop of joy and allow it to thrive! When disappointment raises an unforgettable odor, I sow a future crop of hope despite the smell.

Just as manure boosts the growth in a garden, it is the difficult people, the rancid events, and the putrid circumstances of life that are able to promote the growth of something splendid in me. I am more loving because of the difficult people, stronger due to rancid events, and lovelier because of putrid circumstances. What the enemy meant for evil in my life has been miraculously used to make me stunningly *vibrant*!

It is a well-known fact among horticulturalists that manure or organic matter can actually act as a high-powered growth stimulant in soil. So it is in the garden of your heart. When fetid conditions are thrown upon you, the Master Gardener is more than able to bring forth a bumper crop of rapid growth in spite of the odor. In reality, we should welcome those difficult and unwanted events that will eventually cause exponential growth as we give our lives to the Master.

> *Consider it all joy, my brethren, when you encounter various trials, knowing that the testing of your faith produces endurance. And let endurance have its perfect result, so that you may be perfect and complete lacking in nothing.*　　　　　—James 1:2–4

Planted Not Buried

There are times in life when the darkness surrounds you and the smell reviles you, but at that moment, you must remind yourself that you are *not* buried—you are planted! When you are covered by darkness, remind yourself that inside of you lies a seed of hope, peace, and joy. When life tries to bury you, allow it to be a growing season of your heart. God does a work in the dark places in life that will not happen anywhere else. God will release a treasure of His character in you that will define your calling and propel you into greatness.

> *I will give you the treasures of darkness and hidden wealth of secret places, so that you may know that it is I, the LORD, the God of Israel, who calls you by your name.*　　　　　—Isaiah 45:3

Let hope spring forth from the darkness and joy radiate from the smell. Allow the peace that surpasses all understanding (see Philippians 4:7) enable you to stand strong when darkness is all that you see. What was meant to destroy you could, in fact, be your most abundant growing season of all!

Would you pray with me today:

Lord Jesus, I love You so much. Thank You that I can have joy even when my world is imploding. Thank You that You are with me in every season in life and that You are preparing me for rapid growth. In Jesus's name I pray. Amen.

Rejoicing is not the denial of bad news. It is the bone-deep conviction of news so good that it will one day bring eternal relief to this ailing creation. Rejoicing in the Lord is an audacious act of faith in Christ and a bold defiance against the darkness threatening to engulf us.

—Beth Moore

4

Go Higher!

Finally, as you prepare the rich soil of your heart to grow a fabulous and award-winning array of beauty, there is one more step that must be considered.

If the soil in an actual garden resists improvement after digging deeply to remove rocks and other foreign matter, and if the soil refuses to be improved by the manure that has been mixed into its substance, then the last step that must be taken is that the gardener may resort to raising the garden beds with the use of boxes or frames.

If you believe that the growth of your life has been brittle or nonexistent, then perhaps it is time for you to raise the framework and set your gaze and your heart to a higher reference point.

Worship is the potent discipline that will guarantee your capacity to live a life of satisfying fruit, magnificent flowers, and ravishing sustenance. When you don't like the person you have become, rather than thinking about you, think about Him.

When you are frustrated with the way that you treat people, the words that you speak, and your weakened thought life, begin to place your heart and mind on the wonder of Him.

Only You!

Set your mind on things above, not on the things that are on earth. For you have died and your life is hidden with Christ in God. When Christ, who is our life, is revealed, then you also will be revealed with Him in glory. —Colossians 3:2–4

You are the only one who is able to make this life-altering choice. I cannot set your mind on things above for you. You are the one who must think about what you are thinking about and determine whether or not your thought life is encouraging growth in your life or inhibiting it.

Just as I choose to set the tea kettle on the burner of my stove on any given morning, or set apart time for daily exercise, or set aside money for savings, I must also choose to set my mind high rather than low. I must, I simply must, choose to think about Him even when my life seems to be crumbling.

If I am honest, my mind often doesn't *feel* like thinking about things above, but it insists on ricocheting back to the problems, the pain, and the disappointment. However, as a competent steward of the Word of God, I must remind myself that I don't *get* to do what I *want* to do. The joy of life this side of heaven is that I am *invited to do* what He deems best. What a rare invitation! Why would anyone turn Him down? Who wouldn't want to partner with Him in living a life filled with abundant joy, hope, and peace?

When you choose to set your mind on the things of this earth, you are turning down His vital invitation.

I must remind myself daily that my reference point is not my pain but Him who gives me strength in days of pain. My true north is not the discouragement that ravages my soul but the One who declares, "Take courage! I have overcome the world!" (See John 16:33.) The focal point of my life is not what I see with my natural eye but the One who loves me *"with an everlasting love"* (Jeremiah 31:3).

For as the heavens are higher than the earth, so are My ways higher than your ways and My thoughts than your thoughts.

—Isaiah 55:9

Of course His ways are higher than mine! He is God and I am but a mere human. He is the omniscient Father while I am a weak mortal. If I refuse His thoughtful request to think about Him even while I am slogging through manure, it is the most foolish decision I could make. If I long to create a life of unmatched joy and dynamic hope, then I must go higher in my thought life.

But GOD, dear Lord, I only have eyes for you.

—Psalm 141:8 MSG

High Places of the Heart

My heart is not always a place of beauty; is yours? Often, I have woefully discovered that my heart is the ugliest part of me. I find that I treasure the wrong things and reject that which is honorable. I exalt the temporary and ignore the eternal. I exclaim over the insignificant and grumble about the divine. There is only one cure for a heart like mine: I must take my divided heart to the high places of worship. The first step in our quest to go higher is to think about Him and the second step is to worship Him.

Great is the LORD, and greatly to be praised, in the city of our God, His holy mountain. Beautiful in elevation, the joy of the whole earth, is Mount Zion in the far north, the city of the great King.   —Psalm 48:1–3

You and I were made to be worshippers. We were created to live with our feet planted on terra firma but with our hearts set on heaven. We were designed to be at our best when we choose to worship the King of all kings. Worship turns a weakened heart into a vibrant heart that is miraculously able to pump with a strength denied to many. When I pick up my troubles and travel to the high places where His glory dwells, I discover my true purpose and eternal calling. Charles Spurgeon, a great theologian, Christian author, and preacher from the nineteenth century, has always challenged me with these unforgettable words:

My dear friend, when grief presses you to the dust, worship there.

I will never exhibit His character until I choose to join the earthly choir of resolute singers. I will never be the fruitful harvest of His presence until I choose to worship even when I don't feel like it. When a man or a woman chooses to make the arduous journey up the mountain of worship, despite pain, suffering, and mistreatment, God will meet them in that high place with His strength and with His joy.

There's a day coming when the mountain of GOD's House will be The Mountain—solid, towering over all mountains. All nations will river toward it, people from all over set out for it. They'll say, "Come, let's climb GOD's Mountain, go to the House of the God of Jacob. He'll show us the way he works so we can live the way we're made. —Isaiah 2:2–3 MSG

Would you pray with me today:

Lord Jesus, thank You for calling me to a higher place of worship, to a higher way of thinking and to a higher way of living. Jesus, I don't want to meditate on my human thoughts but I want to fully embrace Your mind and therefore Your heart.

I only have eyes for You, Jesus. In Your blessed name I pray. Amen.

How completely satisfying to turn from our limitations
to a God who has none.
—A. W. Tozer

PART TWO

Suffering with Joy

5

Learning to Love What I Hate

Life is hard, isn't it? Disappointments hammer us ferociously and relentlessly while discouragement bullies us daily. Difficult people refuse to leave us alone and rejection is often a constant companion. There have been hard things in my life that have threatened to crush the very purpose for my existence. I know that you have experienced the *hard* in life as well although yours might look different than mine. I may not understand what you are going through today, but I do know the One who knows your pain and I am intimately acquainted with the One who hears your gut-wrenching cries. In my life, I can assure you, it has been through the deepest pain that God has harvested the most vibrant fruit.

Although we would desire that the ability to live a vibrant life would exclude painful experiences, it just isn't so. The most beautiful gardens and the sweetest fruit in life are often found where joy and sorrow meet.

There are many challenging occurrences in life over which we are powerless. We might even believe that these unwelcome guests are mangling our ability to live a life of beauty and productivity. My friend, absolutely nothing could be further from God's truth! If you feel that you are in a circumstance today that you are unable to do anything about, let me assure you that God wants you to do something with it. He wants you to rename that devastatingly hard place, "Joy." You might not be able to change that place, but you can allow *it* to change *you* to be more like Jesus. He wants you to rediscover Him there.

Worship and Remember

We are not the first Christians to go through difficulties, nor will we be the last. It seems that suffering may actually be a theme in the history of Christianity through the ages.

Two thousand years ago, a man named Peter wrote a beautiful letter to a group of people who were suffering. These Christians, persecuted by the cruel and corrupt ruler Nero, had been driven from their homes and forced to live in alien lands. It is to this group of scattered, broken souls that Peter writes:

Blessed be the God and Father of our Lord Jesus Christ, who according to His great mercy has caused us to be born again to **a living hope** *through the resurrection of Jesus Christ from the dead, to obtain an inheritance which is imperishable and undefiled and will not fade away, reserved in heaven for you, who are protected by the power of God through faith for a salvation ready to be revealed in the last time.* —1 Peter 1:3–5

Peter instantly turns these broken hearts to the life-giving option of praise. Peter breaks out into a written song as his words travel from his heart to the suffering first-century Christians … and to you and me. His call to worship all that is eternally hopeful has not diminished in the two millennia since it was written.

Peter immediately turned the attention of the persecuted sojourners away from the hardships they were facing and defiantly toward all that is ours in Christ Jesus. I have found, in my challenging journey this side of heaven, the vital necessity of determining the direction of my thought life. I can either think about me, or I can think about Him. I can either ponder my disappointment, or I can linger on His hope. I can either meditate on my pain, or I can bask in His promises. I must choose what will fill the thoughts of my days and the words of my prayers. I must choose.

Peter was the cheerleader and the voice of hope to this weary group of pilgrims. Would you allow me to be your cheerleader and your voice of hope today? Would you allow me to remind you of the eternal truths found in the Bible? Would you?

Peter reminded those early Christians to travel through and even beyond the painful days of life. The first lesson that Peter presents is to worship and remember.

When your life collides with human suffering and pain, lift your hands in the air and begin to worship. Break out into a song of faith before the fleeting moment of suffering becomes your reality. Interrupt your disappointment with a melody so rich and so deep that heaven gasps in wonder.

I have learned that I am able to sing and cry at the same time—and I often do. While tears are coursing down my middle-aged cheeks, I raise my voice to the Father and worship Him. When my heart is breaking with the pain only a mother knows, I refuse to let my unique song become a dirge. I will sing in spite of pain, in the face of discouragement, and defy depression.

Peter can't sing for me and I can't sing for you. You must choose to bless the Lord at the worst moment of your life. You must determine that nothing short of death will deny you of the audacious ability to sing in the dark.

After Peter's reminder to bless the Lord, he wrote an unforgettable list of stunning reminders. Peter, in the face of vicious persecution, kept his eyes, his heart, and his mind set firmly on all that Christ has done for us. This is Peter's list of reminders that calls believers to worship rather than to curl up in pain:

- We have been given a great mercy

- We have been born again to a living hope

- The resurrection of Jesus from the dead changed everything for us

- We are protected by the power of God

- We have a faith that leads to salvation

What a list! What an amazing, miraculous expression of all that is ours because of Christ Jesus our Lord. If you are struggling today with difficult circumstances and unfair happenings in your life, would you take the time, like Peter did, to make a list of all that is yours because of Jesus? My list would look something like this:

- No one can take the joy of His presence from me. (Psalm 16:11)

- I am filled with his power. (Ephesians 3:20)

- When I pray according to His will, He hears me. (1 John 5:14)

- He has given a comforting Helper to me. (John 14:16)

- I have His perfect peace. (Isaiah 26:3)

- Greater is He who is in me than he who is in the world. (1 John 4:4)

Something So Good

As I linger peacefully over Peter's list of remembrance, I recall a sermon that I heard when I was just a young woman attending a Christian university in the mid-1970s.

Although many preachers and evangelists of the day received invitations to speak at the biweekly campus chapel service, the student body's most well-loved speaker was always Brother Bob Stamps, the campus chaplain. Brother Bob had an ingenious way of causing the Scriptures to come alive with historical references, enthusiastic delivery, and solid theology.

As a young woman, I thought Peter must have been a lot like Brother Bob, who tackled the issues of the day head-on and was a perpetual source of opinion, wisdom, and rich thinking.

The week after Easter, Brother Bob delivered one of the finest sermons he'd given during the entire four years that I attended this amazing university. As he closed his sermon on the theology of Easter and all that is now ours because the tomb was empty, Bob boldly declared, "We are an Easter people! Something so good has happened to us that nothing can ever really be sad again!"

Our youthful congregation rose to its feet with a collective roar as we closed with the rousing hymn by Robert Lowry, "Up from the Grave He Arose!"

Over the years, I have recalled that particular sermon often and I have pondered the words that I so enthusiastically embraced in my youth. Honestly, there have been days in life when I have vehemently disagreed with Bob's perspective. However, as life marches on and I deepen my relationship with the Man of Sorrows (see Isaiah 53:3), I once again agree with Brother Bob.

I am the beneficiary of a love so rich in measure and so unrelenting in sacrifice that everything else pales in comparison. Like Peter, I will remember and will worship. I am a woman of Easter.

A Living Hope

There is a three-word phrase nestled and nearly hidden amid Peter's call to worship and remember. As you have probably guessed by now, it's the phrase "a living hope." We must not ignore the power of those three small words; we must taste them, digest them, and be restored by them.

Peter and the Holy Spirit were writing to a hopeless world. The Christians had been driven from their homes due to persecution and had no hope of ever returning home, making a productive living, or being reunited with family members. Their hope was dead—stone-cold dead.

And yet strong-willed Peter—once a rugged, burly fisherman who was now a fisher of men (see Mark 1:17)—had the audacity to remind this persecuted and scattered people group that they had been born again to "a living hope"!

I am calling you to the same possibility today.

Embracing a living hope, even in the midst of trying times, is at the very core of living a vibrant life. Hope, by its very definition, is something that has not yet come to pass nor is yet seen. Hope is the clarion call to walk by faith and not by sight. Peter wasn't talking about a dead hope or a stagnant hope; he was cheering every believer in every generation to walk on in *"a living hope."*

Something that is alive grows and gets bigger every day. Something that is alive has a heartbeat and a constant airflow. Something that is alive is meant to be strong and productive. All of this—and more!—is what *"a living hope"* is able to do in the life of someone who has been tormented by the devastation of circumstances.

If you are hoping to win a million dollars in the lottery ... well, that could very well be a dead hope. If you are hoping to wake up tomorrow morning and be ten years younger, that is *definitely* a dead hope. But if you are hoping to be strengthened by the power of God every day of your earthly existence, that is a living hope, indeed! If you are hoping that your son or your daughter will come back to faith in Christ, that, too, is a living hope of the very best kind!

And, of course, the most exciting and vital living hope of all is that someday, we will be in heaven with our Savior and Lord.

Just Do It!

The clarion call across the ages to troubled and broken people is to worship and remember. I can do that; can you? I can set my default to the sure settings of *worship* and *remember.* My tears do not comfort me but worship miraculously has the power to restore and renew. When I choose to rehash my pain and my problems, I weaken myself, but when I recall the goodness of the Lord, I am filled with unstoppable power.

My life, without the determination to worship and remember, will be unable to produce anything of value or worth. However, when I choose to bless the Lord and recall His promises toward me, the vibrant life that He promised washes over me like a restorative waterfall. I am captured by all that He is as I choose to open my mouth and sing.

Would you pray with me today:

Lord Jesus, I love You so much! I thank You right now that I have been born again to a living hope. I thank You for Your great mercy and for Your protection over my life. Lord Jesus, I just love serving You and loving You. In Your precious name I pray. Amen.

Growth in the Christian life depends on
obedience in times of crisis.
—Dr. James Dobson

6

Ridiculous Advice

Peter was never known to be a man who would skirt around a difficult issue or ignore it. Peter had already walked on water, cut off a soldier's ear, and brilliantly preached to the leading religious leaders of the day by the time he wrote his first letter to the persecuted church. Peter was a *man's man* with fish guts under his fingernails and joy in his soul. His vibrant words echo through the ages to a group of people whose very world had fallen apart:

> *In this you greatly rejoice, even though now for a little while, if nec-*
> *essary, you have been distressed by various trials, so that the proof*
> *of your faith, being more precious than gold which is perishable,*
> *even though tested by fire, may be found to result in praise and*
> *glory and honor at the revelation of Jesus Christ.*
>
> —1 Peter 1:6–7

This is the most ridiculous advice that I have ever heard in my life! I am grateful that Peter did at least acknowledge the sincere truth that the people to whom he was writing had been *"distressed by various trials."* However, his words of advice seem contradictory to the expected and healthy response one would expect from people who were dealing with vile persecution. Peter didn't tell them to greatly weep, nor did he coach them to greatly complain. He told the scattered, broken, bullied church, "It's time for you to sing!"

Peter's advice echoes through the centuries and hits a bull's-eye in your life and in my life. You, my friend, will never live a vibrant life without partaking of this masterful and demanding discipline of greatly rejoicing when, in the natural, there is absolutely no reason for you to sing.

However, as people of faith, this must be our default. We must *"greatly rejoice"* when our hearts are broken, when we have been ignored and forgotten, and when we feel like throwing in that infamous towel. We must greatly rejoice. We simply must!

The word for *"rejoice"* that Paul and the Holy Spirit have chosen to use in this life-changing sentence is *agalliao*, which is not used by secular Greek writers. When this word is used in the New Testament, it always describes a deep spiritual joy. It was the word that Mary used in what is known as the Magnificat:

My soul glorifies the Lord and my spirit rejoices in God my Savior. —Luke 1:46–47 NIV

Agalliao was also the response that the Philippian jailer had when he and his entire household chose to believe in God. (See Acts 16:34.)

This type of joy, or rejoicing, is always prompted by a profound spiritual joy. When you know Christ, there is no option other than to greatly rejoice in spite of the trials. When you have embraced a living hope, you must greatly rejoice regardless of your circumstances. The ability to *greatly rejoice* does not come from your personality, your circumstances, or from what is visible. It comes from the deep assurance that God loves us and that He will write the end of our stories well.

Joy and Sorrow

The unlikely combination of *joy* and *sorrow* is a theme from the earliest pages of Scripture. The miraculous blend of joy and sorrow in the life of a believer is a potent recipe for the possibility of living a vibrant life. You may think that stirring joy into sorrow is much like adding oil to water, but it is absolutely not so. Sorrow and joy are a perfect match—a match made in heaven!

You have turned for me my mourning into dancing; You have loosed my sackcloth and girded me with gladness, that my soul may sing praise to You and not be silent. O LORD my God, I will give thanks to You forever. —Psalm 30:11–12

There are some people who know with certainty that joy comes *after* sorrow, but I am one of those audacious yet humble folks who know with certainty that joy comes *with* sorrow. Joy and sorrow are not mutually exclusive; they are holy twins.

We often don't believe that joy and sorrow are simultaneously possible because we don't know what true joy is. Joy is the presence of God. Joy is the atmosphere that surrounds the throne room of the Father. Sorrows do not exclude the presence of God, which is the very reason why joy and sorrow are a perfect fit for one another. Your sorrow requires the joy of the Lord to refine it, cope with it, and then to move beyond it.

Joy is not the absence of trouble, but the presence of Christ.
—William Vander Hoven

We mistakenly believe that experiencing an earthly sorrow is the reason why we are unable to live with a vibrant faith or a vibrant peace. We presume that sorrow is the one ingredient that causes us to live a barren life, or to wander along the dry sands of the desert. However, when a person is bold enough to mix even a teaspoon of joy into a cup of sorrow, a miracle begins to happen! And when this bold person begins to add joy in greater degrees to their sorrow? Why, the results are nothing short of astounding!

Life is renewed and hope is restored where joy and sorrow meet. Strength is found and peace is discovered as joy and sorrow are stirred together. A vibrant life is possible, my friend, when you choose to greatly rejoice even while being distressed by various trials.

I will turn their mourning into joy.   —Jeremiah 31:13

Anguish is turned into joy when a large dose of rejoicing is splashed upon the dry sands of sorrow. Mourning becomes a miracle when a man or a woman begins to sing in spite of their human pain. It was the advice of Peter to a people group deeply grieving and it is his advice to you today.

The Angels and Me

I have always deeply longed to have a beautiful voice. I have taken voice lessons from time to time, but my voice has never developed in the manner that I wish it would. While it is true that I can carry a tune and even sing harmony with the best of them, I have more of a *choir voice* than a solo voice.

I have developed a few vocal heroines over the years. I have always wished that I could sing like Sandi Patty, Celine Dion, or Barbra Streisand in her prime. When I was young, I always wanted to sing like Karen Carpenter. How I wish I had been given the pipes of Renee Fleming! The truth is, I would have been satisfied with just a tenth of any one of their vocal gifts.

However, I am fully assured that I *do* have a voice and I have been given a song to sing.

I have discovered that the most beautiful song that has ever been given to me was given to me in the valley. There is no angel that can sing the song that I have learned in the valley. The voice lessons that I have been given in the wilderness have honed my voice and refined my song until it has become a symphony of praise.

And I alone sing it.

I believe that anyone can sing on the mountaintop of life, but when the Father leads us through the valley, it is for the rare experience of learning to sing the song of His heart.

Anyone can sing the song of celebration, and I will sing that song as well.

However, the song that is taught in the wilderness has a rich quality that no other song has.

Let's read some words that Peter wrote two centuries ago:

---

*Concerning this salvation, the prophets, who spoke of the grace that was to come to you, searched intently and with the greatest care, trying to find out the time and circumstances to which the Spirit of Christ in them was pointing when he predicted the sufferings of the Messiah and the glories that would follow. It was revealed to them that they were not serving themselves but you, when they spoke of the things that have now been told you by those who have preached the gospel to you by the Holy Spirit sent from heaven. **Even angels long** to look into these things.* —1 Peter 1:10–12 NIV

The angels long to sing the chorus that you and I learn during our days of suffering. The angels gasp when you and I break out into song this side of heaven. What a humbling yet thrilling realization! I was born to sing so that the angels could listen to my song, a song that they will never be able to sing.

While it is painfully true that I may never sing like Sandi, or Celine, or Barbra, or Renee, or even like Karen, it is at the same time gloriously true that the angels wish that they could sing like *me*.

What Happens Next

If you can sing even when the tears are rolling down your face and the heaves of pain are enormous, what happens next may just be the greatest miracle of all.

Peter declares that when you rejoice in a trial, your faith is strengthened and purified. Your faith in the Lord Jesus Christ will become a brilliant demonstration of power and joy. Did you know that your faith is the most valuable commodity of your entire life? Your faith is more expensive than your car, your home, your education, or any other valuables that you might have stored away. And when you greatly rejoice even while in the fires of life, your faith increases in value.

Gold must be tested by a searing fire before an exact value can be placed upon it—and so it is with your faith.

Your faith, as your most treasured spiritual commodity, must go through the fire for its significance to be realized in your life. Suffering or trials were never meant to extract strength from our lives, but were designed to increase the strength of our faith.

Trials don't last forever and earthly gold is perishable but our faith is eternal and our song is unending.

The result of worshipping and remembering in a trial is that I am incredibly filled with an unstoppable power; the result of greatly rejoicing during days of suffering is that He reveals Himself to me in that place of pain. As my song drowns out the temporary trial, the melody of my ordinary life will grow louder, more potent, and even more stunning.

Would you pray with me today:

Lord Jesus, You are worthy of my highest praise! I thank You for turning my mourning into dancing and my sorrow into joy. Father, I praise You that because I have You, no sorrow is able to steal my joy. In Jesus's wonderful name I pray. Amen.

Sorrow and celebration can coexist authentically, and giving ourselves permission to have both is incredibly freeing.
—Lysa TerKeurst

7

A Cup of Tea with Peter

I have always longed to learn from some of the heroes and heroines of my faith. Men and women such as Mother Teresa, Billy Graham, and Darlene Rose are just a few of the people I have desired to spend time, with even though they no longer live on earth.

One day not long ago, an instinctive and uninvited thought came to my mind: *I so wish that I could talk to Elisabeth Elliot about this.* When that random thought crossed my mind, Elisabeth had been in heaven nearly five years, not to mention the fact that I had never met her in person when she was alive. I realized in that moment that I had a problem. My problem was that I had enough bravado to even *imagine* that someone like Elisabeth would spend time with me.

I have wanted to pick Ruth Graham's brain from time to time and to have a cup of tea with Corrie ten Boom and just to touch Billy Sunday's Bible. I have deeply desired that in some sense, their anointing and wisdom would rub off on me.

As I bring my hopes and longings into the reality of my life, the wonder of it all is that I get to experience the anointing and wisdom of the men who have written the Bible. So for today, I will learn from Peter.

An Uncommon Heart

Peter was a common man with an uncommon heart. He had been with Jesus for three years and that experience had changed everything for this Galilean. Peter wrote one of the most beautiful books in the entire New Testament and we are the beneficiaries of his words and life today.

And though you have not seen Him, you love Him, and though you do not see Him now, but believe in Him, you greatly rejoice with joy inexpressible and full of glory, obtaining as the outcome of your faith the salvation of your souls. —1 Peter 1:8–9

Peter had seen Jesus in the flesh! What a rare and historic experience that had been! The young man who had probably never traveled farther than the shores of Galilee had been in a close friendship with the God of eternity in the flesh. Peter had been there when the loaves and fish had been multiplied, had seen Lazarus raised from the dead, and had run into the empty tomb of Jesus. It is no wonder that Peter would later give his life for the gospel of Jesus Christ.

Peter was amazed that these early Christians, who had been brutally persecuted for their faith, loved Jesus even though they had never seen Him in the flesh. He applauded their great faith in a Man they had never even met! What an extraordinary group of people!

You and I are in the same category as these amazing pilgrims. We have never seen Jesus and yet we love Him. We did not experience walking along the dusty roads of Galilee and Judea with Jesus, nor did we hear Him cry out on the cross—yet we still believe.

Peter is writing to *us*. His words travel confidently across the years and find a resting place in me. I am breathless at his advice and wisdom. I will make it a priority to obey the man who walked with Jesus in the flesh.

Not Once, But Twice

I had a mother who was a stickler for details and expected exact obedience instantly. If my proper and loving mother had to ask her trio of lively children to obey a second time, we knew that discipline was sure to follow. My mom believed that instructing children only once in a certain behavior was more than enough.

I am so thankful that Peter is not as exacting as my mom. Peter admonished these displaced and discouraged believers once again to *"greatly rejoice,"* this time urging them to do so *"with joy inexpressible and full of glory."* Wow! I can barely keep my soul from singing even as I type these words!

As a woman of the twenty-first century, I am charged with the same behavior that all of those who have gone before me have been commanded to do. When I raise my voice in joyful singing, I am joining the army of believers in all generations past who have determined to sing instead of complain. What a joyful noise we make! What a mighty choir of warriors we are!

The joy that is ours as believers in Christ is simply inexpressible. There are no human words that are able to communicate the joy that is ours because of Him. There are no adjectives or adverbs that have the capacity to describe the incomprehensible joy that belongs to those who belong to Jesus.

We sing when we are together and we sing when we are alone. We rejoice when life is easy and we rejoice louder when life is hard. We raise our voices in praise when we are sick and when we are well. We belt out a glorious hymn in abundance and roar louder in lack. And as we sing, we join the harmony of the saints of the kingdom who have traveled this dusty road before us.

Our joy might be inexpressible, but we will spend the rest of our human lives endeavoring to express it. We will not waste one minute or one hour focusing on our pain or disappointment, but we will sing for the world to hear. Thank you, Peter, for speaking into my life across the sands of time. Can you hear me singing, Peter?

Would you pray with me:

Lord Jesus, thank You for the joy that You have given to me. I am unable to describe the joy that You have given to me, but I know Your joy is real and I am so grateful for it. Father God, I love You so much today and every day. In Jesus's powerful name I pray. Amen.

The secret of joy is Christ in me, not me in
a different set of circumstances.
—Elisabeth Elliot

PART THREE

The Secret Garden of the Soul

8

You Are God's August

August is a miraculous and marvelous month. It teeters between summer and fall with the longest and loveliest days of the year. It is the month of wildflowers in glorious bloom, sunsets vibrant in the sleepy dusk, and vegetable gardens abundant beyond measure. August sings in chrysanthemums, boasts in bachelor buttons, and shouts with sunflowers bending in the afternoon sunshine.

There Is No Place Like a Garden

Often, during the month of August, I spend a few weeks with a friend. She is actually more like a sister and loves a family garden nearly as much as I do. Every afternoon of the August fortnight that we are together, we wander out to her enormous garden and delightfully choose what to eat for dinner that night. While spending time with her, I became an expert at cutting lettuce, gently squeezing ripe tomatoes, and eyeing the color and size of cucumbers. I even discovered how to find a pepper or two underneath the verdant growth of her garden.

However, the greatest pleasure of my two-week garden experience happened when we placed the ripe vegetables and fruit of her garden into baskets and then gave the produce to others. What a treasure it is to share from the bounty of one's garden and spread the riches of the earth with others!

Certainly the best part of my annual visit with her is the day that we set aside to preserve the yearly abundance. Under her tutelage, I became a veritable virtuoso at canning tomatoes and making a smashing dill pickle relish. The hamburger pickles that we developed are nearly legendary. But the highlight of the long day for me was the moment when we canned peaches fresh from the trees. We knew that the labor of our love was not only going to feed our families for the winter, but would also be welcome gifts for our friends.

Oh, how I love the array of colors that are visible through the formerly empty jars. And just to think—she grew it and we canned it! There is nothing quite like the delight that results from an August agricultural endeavor.

August is God's show and tell of His unmatched creativity and strategic forethought of provision for His children. August is the moment of the year when all of creation shouts a resounding cheer to the One who created the very first garden in history.

A Perfectly Wonderful Word

As I remember those sweet days of walking the rows of my friend's garden and as I never ceased to be amazed at the plentitude thereof, the word *flourish* seems to fill the sense of my heart.

Isn't *flourish* a perfectly wonderful word? Let's linger on it for a bit, and unpack the joy and hope of this lovely word. I can assure you that this will not be the only time in this book that we will dawdle over the meaning of *flourish*. You will discover, as I have, that the ability to flourish is a prerequisite to living a vibrant life.

Let's pause among the sacred pages of the Bible to read the thoughts of the Holy Spirit concerning this perfectly wonderful word.

---

*The righteous man will **flourish** like the palm tree, he will grow like a cedar in Lebanon. Planted in the house of the L*ORD*, they will **flourish** in the courts of our God. They will still yield fruit in old age; they shall be full of sap and very green, to declare that the L*ORD *is upright; He is my rock, and there is no unrighteousness in Him.* —Psalm 92:12–15

Isn't this wonderful news? You are God's August! You were created to flourish in the same manner that gardens are able to do so at the peak of their performance.

God made you to flourish and to inexhaustibly thrive. He did not create you with the purpose of dying on the vine of life. He spiritually designed you for emotional and spiritual abundance in every season of your life.

The plan of the Master Gardener was that you would never be shriveled up emotionally, or trampled upon by anger, depression, or worry. God's intent was that you would not live a brittle life. Instead, you, as His vibrant creation, would live a life that flourishes.

Many definitions of the word *flourish* can be found in dictionaries, encyclopedias, and gardening manuals, but the one that most deeply resonates within this spiritual gardener's heart is this particular one: "*To receive life from outside yourself, creating vitality within yourself and producing blessing beyond yourself!*"

When you receive life from the Father, it will create a vitality on the inside of you that is contagious and fruitful! Who wouldn't want that?! But the purpose of the extraordinary growth inside of you is not just for you because it is intended to bless other people in your world. His life helps you to flourish and then share your life with others.

In the ancient Hebrew, *flourish* always refers to something or someone that is growing beyond an average expectation of growth. It was meant to describe a person or a plant that was growing and producing fruit in an extraordinary fashion. *Flourish* in the Hebrew paints a word picture of a plant that is destined to grow abundantly regardless of the climate or drought.

The psalmist declares, "*The righteous man will flourish like the palm tree.*" If the Bible uses the word *righteous* to describe a person, it means that this person has willfully chosen to connect himself or herself to God. It does not imply that the person is perfect, but it *does* mean that he or she has chosen to put on God's imputed righteousness.

You will flourish, then, in direct proportion to your connection with God.

If you choose to bask in His presence on a daily basis and spend time in the Word and in prayer, your life will be a grand display of the growth that comes from your connection to His righteousness.

Delicious Fruit

If you long to be God's August and if your desire is to flourish and thereby produce delicious fruit for others, you must ask yourself a vital question: "To whom or to what are you choosing to be connected?"

Many Christians are more connected to the pain of their past than they are to the reality of His presence on a daily basis. If you hope to flourish emotionally, it matters very much whether or not you read your Bible every day. If you hope to be a vibrant display of the fruits of the Holy Spirit, it matters very much whether or not you worship in spite of disappointment or pain. If you long to share the abundance of your Christian walk with others, it matters very much whether or not you pray for those who have been unkind to you.

You will begin to grow by leaps and bounds both spiritually and emotionally when you daily receive life from the Father. The fruits of the Spirit will miraculously make you into someone who has the temperament and personality of God. When you choose to be in vital connection with Jesus on a daily basis, the life that you will receive will grow you into the person who God had in mind the day that He created you.

You must work in tandem with God in the garden of your heart. Your emotional responses to the climate around you must reflect the truth that you are in deep and rich connection with Him. The Father gives to you what you could never instigate in your own strength. You can't do it without Him and He won't do it without you!

You are God's August! It is a magnificent time for you to produce such a unique abundance in your life that the world stops and takes note—and don't be surprised if it takes a bite or two of the August that is you.

Would you pray with me today:

Lord Jesus, I want to flourish in Your garden. Father, would You use my life as a demonstration of how wonderful a life can be that is cultivated by You? I pray that others would come to me, eat the fruit of the Holy Spirit, and be satisfied and filled in Jesus's faithful name. Amen.

⌒

We might think we are nurturing our garden, but of course it's our garden that is really nurturing us.
—Jenny Uglow

9

Unseasonably Abundant

One of the highlights of my year is an extended winter vacation to Mobile, Alabama, where the tea is sweet, the magnolias are fragrant, and the moss hangs low from the stately oak trees.

My lifetime mentor and friend, Carolyn, always made sure that I was able to escape the vicious winters in Buffalo, New York, with a sunny respite in the gracious city of Mobile. Now, although I no longer live where winter is frigid, Carolyn continues to fly me to her home, surround me with her wisdom, and shower me with southern hospitality in January or February.

A year or two ago, when I went to Mobile for my annual visit, the temperatures soared into the high 80s every single day! Generally, during the winter months, the temperatures in Mobile hover in the 50s and low 60s, but this particular year, it was more like May or June. Oh, how I loved it!

Everyone, including the local weatherman, continued to proclaim that the temperatures were unseasonal. Carolyn, her husband Bernard, and I watched the news every evening and just grinned at each other. Bernard would shake his balding head and say, "Carol, it is never like this in February. Never!"

Finally, after nearly a week of balmy weather, Bernard exclaimed, "Carol, I am convinced that God has done this just for you! He knows how much you hate winter in Buffalo and so He is restoring your soul in the sunshine and warmth."

The truth is that I would have been delighted to visit Mobile even during 50-degree weather; it was much preferable to the arctic blast of winter in Buffalo. But God did something unusual that year; He blessed me with something unseasonal and unexpected. My Father, who knows me so well, was delighted to present me with the temperatures of spring and early summer even though it was abnormal in the natural. He delighted me with something unexplainable in His rich and imaginative way.

As I was walking one afternoon through streets that were framed by azaleas, I was sweating and rejoicing as I thanked my Father for the sunshine and summer temperatures. I thanked Him profusely that He had done it just for me. I showered Him with heartfelt gratitude for the unseasonable warmth because I knew that it should have been at least 25 degrees cooler on this afternoon walk.

I felt the Lord whisper to my heart in the middle of my personal hymn of praise, "Carol, I gave you this weather because I want you to think about what it means to be unseasonably abundant. I want you to feel the delight of something unexpected and unexplainable. Carol, I want you to live a life that is known as unseasonably abundant and share that delight with others."

I immediately responded to Him with the very first thought that came to my mind, "Well ... that will preach!"

He gently responded to my oblivious heart, "Carol, I am not talking about preaching but I am referring to the way that you live. I want you to live an unseasonably abundant lifestyle!"

Delighted and Firm

One of the very first Scriptures that I memorized as a young child was Psalm 1. This life-giving psalm has guided me through many challenging days in life and continues to be a source of both comfort and instruction.

How blessed is the man [woman] *who does not walk in the counsel of the wicked, nor stand in the path of sinners, nor sit in the seat of scoffers! But his* [her] *delight is in the law of the* LORD, *and in His law he* [she] *meditates day and night. He* [She] *will be like a tree firmly planted by streams of water, which yields its fruit in its season and its leaf does not wither; and in whatever he* [she] *does, he* [she] *prospers.* —Psalm 1:1–3

God has decreed that we, as His children, are to live an unseasonal lifestyle that is abnormal to the world's expectations. It is His divine will and holy pleasure to offer sustenance and vibrancy to us even during the difficult days of life. As God's children, we are to be *Exhibit A* of how people are able to live when they attach themselves to the perpetual life flow of the Word of God.

Just making this one simple choice of determining to read the Bible and then thinking about the Word every day of our life on earth changes our lives from unstable to stable, and from arid to abundant. When you and I firmly remain close to the refreshing truth of the Word of God, we will bloom when others are withering, and we will thrive when others are languishing. We will be unseasonably abundant!

When I am consistently in the Word of God, I notice quiet behavioral changes in my life that are subtle and even unconscious. For instance, when I read my Bible regularly for a week or two, and I allow the truth to nestle down deeply within me, I will suddenly realize that my husband is not getting on my nerves anymore. What happened to me?! The Word happened to me!

Or, perhaps I have been weepy due to financial struggles or loneliness, and one day, I wake up and realize that I feel strong and vibrant. What happened to me?! The Word happened to me!

The Word of God is able to fertilize our lives in such a manner that we are the beneficiaries of an unseasonable abundance!

Blessed and Planted

Perhaps anxiety or worry has caused you to live an unfruitful or parched life; maybe your tendency to default to fear rather than to faith has resulted in a barren existence even during the easy days of life.

Blessed is the man [woman] *who trusts in the* LORD *and whose trust is the* LORD. *For he* [she] *will be like a tree planted by the water, that extends its roots by a stream and will not fear when the heat comes; but its leaves will be green. And it will not be anxious in a year of drought nor cease to yield fruit.* —Jeremiah 17:7–8

As you choose to put your whole trust in the Lord and as you hold worry and anxiety at bay, you will notice that the fruit of your life is suddenly juicy and apparent. Rather than caving in to fear, declare your trust in the God who loves you and cares for you. Remind yourself daily that His ways are indeed higher and wiser than yours could ever be. (See Isaiah 55:9.)

Often in life we are tempted to put our trust in things of this world, such as the political system, increased finances, or the acceptance of others. However, all of those arenas in life are temporary and have no eternal blessing for us. We must place all of our faith in the Father who is able to offer an unseasonable abundance in His greenhouse of growth.

When you snuggle up to Him in an attitude of complete and submissive surrender, your roots will begin to go deeply into the plans and promises of God Almighty. Even when life is difficult and it seems like you are in the desert of circumstances, your life will remain vibrant and even fruitful. You will continue to yield joy when everyone else is discouraged, and you will be perpetually kind when others are cruel. You will be peaceful even when your life is being storm-tossed by ferocious situations, and you will be patient when it seems as if your prayers are being placed on hold.

How does this happen? What does it take to continue to yield fruit even when there is no reason for that to happen naturally? It happens when a man or a woman is bold enough to trust the Lord for daily sustenance, for sure protection, and for future stability. It happens when a person is more attached to the promises of God than they are to the pain of their past. It happens.

Would you pray with me today:

Lord, I thank You that You have enabled me to live an unseasonably abundant life. Lord, I thank You that even when the storms of life come, I am filled with the fruit of the Holy Spirit. Lord, because I have You and You have me, I am filled with great joy that even when I am walking through the wilderness, it is You who enables me to continue to grow fruit in my life. In Jesus's name I pray. Amen.

In God's garden of grace, even a broken tree can bear fruit.
—Rick Warren

10

Two Choices

Let me make this incredibly easy for you. There are two vital choices that are linked together ... yet they are different. You must determine how you will respond to these choices before joy is allowed to knock on your door and before holy purpose holds your hand in friendship. You must decide:

- Will I continue to trust the Lord when I hate my circumstances?
- Will I continue to be a blessing to others even when my life is hard?

Perpetual Trust

Stamped on American currency is the phrase, "In God we trust." I am not sure that Congress would verify that same phrase today, but at the birth of our nation, those four words were the foundational motto of our founding fathers. Trust has always been a foundational issue.

We all must determine where we will place our trust, just like the founders of America did more than two hundred years ago. Trust is a foundational issue in all of our lives, whether you are a stay-at-home mom or a corporate attorney. Trust is the building block of a glorious life whether you live in China or in Chicago. Trust is a prerequisite to all that is noble and magnificent. If you don't make this one vital decision—to put all of your trust in the Lord—it will impact every area of your life.

You might think that you really don't trust anyone or anything, but that supposition deserves a rebuttal. We *all* trust someone or something. We trust banks to protect our money and we trust doctors to keep us healthy. We trust mechanics to fix our cars and we trust teachers to educate our children. We trust pilots to fly planes safely and accountants to complete our taxes error-free.

However, there are times in life when we are tempted to place our trust in the wrong things, which holds enormous consequences for a believer in Christ.

Thus says the LORD, *"Cursed is the man who trusts in mankind and makes flesh his strength, and whose heart turns away from the* LORD. *For he will be like a bush in the desert and will not see when prosperity comes, but will live in stony wastes in the wilderness, a land of salt without inhabitant. Blessed is the man who trusts in the* LORD *and whose trust is the* LORD. *For he will be like a tree planted by the water, that extends its roots by a stream and will not fear when the heat comes; but its leaves will be green, and it will not be anxious in a year of drought nor cease to yield fruit."*
—Jeremiah 17:5–8

According to Jeremiah, there is a guaranteed blessing for a person who trusts the Lord completely; conversely, there is a devastating consequence for a man or a woman who chooses not to trust the Lord.

As you walk through life this side of heaven, there will multiple moments in which you need to make a choice. It can be expressed in several different ways, but in reality, it is all one choice:

+ Will I choose to trust the Lord or not?

+ Will I try to control the situation without consulting the Lord?

+ Will I surrender my will to His higher plan?

+ Will I listen to man's opinions more than to God's wisdom?

+ Do I think that I have a better idea than God?

Your answer to any of those questions reflects the level of trust that you have in your Father and in your Creator. When you choose not to trust Him, but to place your feelings and desires above His will and His way, there is a price that you will be required to pay. The prophet Jeremiah warns that your life will be like a parched, brittle bush in the desert, oblivious to the blessings of the Lord. In case you didn't realize it, most bushes actually are unable to grow in the desert. And you, my friend, will not be able to grow without a heart that is filled with trust for your loving Father. The atmosphere of your life will not be vibrant, nor will it produce anything healthy. The wilderness will be your chosen habitat and there will be no potential for growth in your life. How I pray that you will not find yourself in those living conditions!

It just takes one decision to change your environment from a wilderness to a greenhouse. When you choose to trust in the Lord, even during the most difficult days of your life, the blessing will be enormous.

A Critical Phrase

Jeremiah declared, through the unction of the Holy Spirit, "*Blessed is the man who* **trusts in** *the* LORD *and whose trust* **is** *the* LORD." This is one critical phrase that cannot be ignored in our quest to live a life filled with the vitality of Christ. The words of Jeremiah are compelling in that he uses the word *trust* in two different ways.

The first, "*trusts in the Lord,*" is expressed by the Hebrew word *batach*, which can mean "to confide in anyone, to set one's hope and confidence upon any one." It also means "to be secure, to fear nothing for oneself."

When you *trust in the Lord*, you have set your hope and confidence wholly on the Lord. Because you have chosen to make this dynamic choice, you know that you are secure and that you have nothing to fear. If you are still dealing with fear issues in your life, I can assure you that you have not yet placed all of your trust in the Lord.

The second way in which Jeremiah uses the word *trust* is to tell us that our trust must *be* the Lord. *Mibtach*, the Hebrew word used in the second part of Jeremiah's statement, means "sure and firm hope or confidence." Although the phrases are very similar in meaning and can be translated in much the same manner, Jeremiah knew that it was imperative to call believers in God to both place their trust in Him and to make Him their source of trust.

The blessing of choosing to put our trust in the Lord is one that we have read about earlier in other verses. When you put all of your trust in God, not in yourself and not in the systems of the world, you will be like a tree planted by a bubbling, gurgling stream, which will cause you to have nothing to fear when the searing seasons of life come your way. Circumstances will be no match for your overwhelming trust in your good, good Father. You will be so aware of Him and of His care for you that the physical conditions of your life will have no impact on your growing season at all.

When a situational drought comes your way or when you walk through desert-like experiences, you will still be growing in your faith, your hope, and your joy. When others are parched and shriveled by the heat of circumstances, you won't be anxious about your life; you will be filled with enough kindness, goodness, and peace to share with others. That's the kind of life that I want to live, don't you?

And remember, there is only one way to exhibit that type of lifestyle and it is through living a life of wholehearted trust in the Father. God can bless you more abundantly than you could ever imagine when you choose to surrender the control of your life into His capable and faithful hands.

Grace Beyond Ability

I believe that when we trust God wholeheartedly, just as Jeremiah has encouraged us to do, it impacts our actions in life. When we trust God with our time, we are able to serve others with more enthusiasm. When we trust God with our children, we are not fraught with worry and fear. When we trust God with our finances, we are able to give generously.

God's grace is the fertilizer that can turn our "not enough" into "more than enough." I believe that God cheers us on even when the fires of affliction are searing and there is no visible protection. God's grace added to our insufficiency becomes a verdant place of growth when we fertilize it with generosity.

Often when life is hard, it is tempting to withdraw from serving others and even from the call to benevolence. When all you see is a barren wasteland of existence, it is easy to justify taking care of yourself rather than taking care of others. When your bills go unpaid, it becomes increasingly difficult to continue to give to the kingdom of Christ.

Let's read about a people group who were greatly impoverished and yet who chose to give beyond their ability. These believers gave generously, cheerfully, and abundantly. As you read these verses, examine your own heart toward giving:

Now, brethren, we wish to make known to you the grace of God which has been given in the churches of Macedonia, that in a great ordeal of affliction their abundance of joy and their deep poverty overflowed in the wealth of their liberality. For I testify that according to their ability, and beyond their ability, they gave of their own accord, begging us with much urging for the favor of participation in the support of the saints, and this, not as we had expected, but they first gave themselves to the Lord and to us by the will of God. —2 Corinthians 8:1–5

There is a theme that is developing in our quest to live a vibrant life even when the floodwaters are high, when the flames are searing, and when the desert is endless. The motif that is apparent is that we choose how we will live even when we can't control the climate of our lives. The foundation of our life is not created by our circumstances or the situations in which we find ourselves, but rather in the definitive and resolute choices that we make.

We have learned from Psalm 1 that one's ability to blossom in life is directly connected to the delight that a person extracts from the Word of

God. In Jeremiah, the Holy Spirit clearly pointed out that one's ability to continue to produce fruit is linked to the level of trust that a person embraces. And finally, from Paul and the Macedonian church, we learn the lovely lesson of giving in spite of lack. These poor, nearly destitute believers engaged in sacrificial giving. They wanted to help others in spite of their own poverty.

Although this church was afflicted, they revealed an abundance of joy. The believers at Macedonia gave richly and generously even though they had a deep need themselves.

Your ability to live a life of uncommon hope and irrepressible joy is not linked to your circumstances, but it is linked to your choices. So many people slog through their time on this earth expecting a life of beauty to be handed to them while others are determined to create a life of beauty in spite of their pain. There are folks who feel entitled to kindness while there are others who go about simply *being* kind. There are people who presume that every circumstance in life will result in easy living and people whose chief goal is to make the lives of others easier.

Which group do you find yourself in? It's a valid question that deserves an honest answer.

Would you pray with me today:

Lord, help me to make the lives of others easier. Jesus, would You give me the power and the desire to be kind everywhere I go and to everyone I meet? Jesus, I offer myself to You today for use in Your unshakable kingdom. In Jesus's wonderful name I pray. Amen.

I am not moved by what I see.
I am moved only by what I believe.
—Smith Wigglesworth

11

The Glory of You

Oone early autumn afternoon, I was invited to a delightful luncheon in a southern city in which I was speaking. The women at the luncheon were honoring a young woman who had written a powerful book on breaking free from jihad. This group felt that it would be beneficial for me to encourage the novice author in her faith and in her writing ability. They had sent her very well-written book to me prior to the luncheon and I had simply devoured it! It was a riveting page-turner and I was thrilled to be able to pray for and encourage this extraordinary young woman.

We met at a quiet restaurant and sat at a large table. When my hosts and I arrived at the restaurant, we were surprised to be greeted by a wonderfully creative woman who had reached the restaurant before us. She had brought a gorgeous flowing vine from her garden. The stems and leaves of the vine were long-reaching and filled the entire table at which we sat. It went from one end of the table to the other and streamed down the sides. Our artistic friend explained that she had brought this effusive trailing plant to the luncheon because its flowers only bloomed one day a year.

Since this was the day that they had decided to blossom, she didn't want to miss it! So she cut off long sections of the creeping, flowering greenery, placed it in several different jars of water, and then brought it with her. (And yes, in case you are wondering, it was more than just a little strange.)

We found ourselves gently placing the shoots and leaves of the trailing plant to one side of our plates so that they didn't mix with our food.

Now, let me assure you that the blossoms were utterly beautiful. However, I couldn't help but think to myself, *What a waste! I would never want to be a flower that only bloomed once a year! Oh! How I want to be the type of flower that blooms 365 days a year not once every 365 days!*

I long to live a life of irrepressible hope and unquenchable joy. I believe that the Lord deeply desires for the fruit of our lives to be glorious and stunningly apparent in all seasons, in all conditions, in all situations, and in all climates. Nothing, absolutely nothing, should render us fruitless or barren. You, my friend, were meant to bloom without ceasing. The glory of your life is not determined by storms, climate, soil, or by the geography of your life experience. The glory of your life is determined by Him!

Faithfulness, Righteousness, and Thanksgiving

So often, in our attempt to live a life that honors God and produces winsome fruit, we feel alone. We think no one notices our righteous choices. We might even be tempted to believe that faithfulness is archaic. The prophet Isaiah knew that God's people would need encouragement in their arduous quest to honor God. Isaiah offered words of hope nearly 3,000 years ago that still resonate today.

Listen to me, you who pursue righteousness, who seek the LORD: *look to the rock from which you were hewn and to the quarry from which you were dug.* —Isaiah 51:1

Isaiah had a strong word for people in every generation who choose to seek the Lord and he began his encouragement with the phrase, *"Listen to me."* Isaiah wants your attention before he speaks. I want to rouse you today to lean into the wisdom of Isaiah because it just might be the source of strength for which you have been aching.

In the phrase, *"Look to the rock from which you were hewn and to the quarry from which you were dug,"* Isaiah was, in effect, saying, "Look how far you have come!" He was reminding seekers of God and pursuers of righteousness that they should measure their lives by the growth that has taken place. This is not bad advice for those of us today who long to live a powerful life. Rather than be discouraged by minor setbacks or slight mistakes, remind yourself who you used to be *without* Christ and who you have become *with* Him. What a wonderful comparison!

Look to Abraham your father and to Sarah who gave birth to you in pain; when he was but one I called him, then I blessed him and multiplied him. —Isaiah 51:2

Abraham was only one simple man who stayed faithful to his Creator. And yet, we must never overlook what a massive impact Abraham has had on generations of the people of God! Abraham believed the promise of God when, in the natural, there was no reason to believe. His trust was massive and immovable!

Sarah gave birth in pain but the blessing was immeasurable. The product of the pain of your life may hold a rich harvest of grace for you as well. Your pain may lead to a blessing that will resound through history.

The voice of Isaiah is calling across the ages, "Hey, you men and women of faith of the twenty-first century, listen to me right now! Look at Abraham. Learn by his example how to follow God with a relentless faith and with an unshakable trust."

Isaiah is making an invincible case for the harvest that can come from one solitary life. The God of Abraham is the God of you! When you choose to live faithfully and righteously, in the face of fierce opposition, God takes note. The Lord will fertilize your seeds of faithfulness with His divine power and you, like Abraham and Sarah, will be honored by the Father in exuberant and bountiful ways.

Incomparable Hope

Indeed, the LORD *will comfort Zion; He will comfort all her waste places. And her wilderness He will make like Eden, and her desert like the garden of the* LORD*; joy and gladness will be found in her, thanksgiving and the sound of a melody.* —Isaiah 51:3

The beauty of this Scripture is so stirring that it causes my heart to ache with inexpressible hope. We serve the God of all comfort, who takes pleasure in comforting His people. When you are in a barren or dry season in life, He comes to you—not to accuse or condemn, but to comfort you. He comes to whisper reassuring words in your ears and to place His loving arms around you. He wipes away your tears and heals the broken places in you.

What you suppose is a season of waste in your life, He can turn into a lush and prolific garden filled with delicious fruit and exotic flowers. He can take the driest, most arid season of your entire life and turn it into a place where you and He fellowship together intimately. His garden is not only beautiful, it is also the place of sweet companionship with your Savior.

When the children of God were delivered from the bondage of the Egyptians, they were on their way to God's Promised Land. However, because they murmured and complained, they spent forty long years in the scorching heat of the wilderness. Even there, God's children received complete provision. You can rest assured that the wilderness can be a place of growth and a place to learn trust and even contentment.

You may think that you are forgotten in the wilderness and are withered in the desert, but when He arrives, so does joy. In His presence *"is fullness of joy"* (Psalm 16:11); you don't get Him without joy and you don't get joy without Him. What a precious promise! The climate of your life is revolutionized and transformed by His presence and the gladness that He brings with Him. In the desert of your life, the sound is lyrical and symphonic. The song that He gives drowns out the howling winds of misfortune and the echoing growls of the gathering beasts. He gives a perpetual melody that is not silenced by pain, by storms, or by threats. His melody prevails in you!

Would you pray with me today:

Lord Jesus, I want to bloom more than one day a year! Lord, would You fertilize my life so that I will flourish and bloom even during the dry seasons of life? I long to bring glory to Your name through everything that I do and everything that I say. In Jesus's perfect name I pray. Amen.

⌒

Either He will shield you from suffering or
He will give you unfailing strength to bear it.
Be at peace, then, and put aside all anxious thoughts.
—Francis de Sales

12

Every Day

There is a very small book filled with wonder and power tucked away near the closing pages of the Old Testament. Don't be fooled by the length of the book of Habakkuk. Although it is only three short chapters long, in it lies some of the most profound truths of the entire Old Testament.

Habakkuk was a man on a tireless search for truth. He was devastated by what he saw happening in the world around him, so he decided to pose the difficult questions of life to his God. Habakkuk wasn't cocky or bitter when he asked these questions, but his heart was indeed breaking. This man asked questions that perhaps you and I are afraid to bring into the throne room of the Father. Habakkuk was insistent on knowing why there was evil in the world and why the wicked seem to be so blessed.

God answered this tender man with a profusion of wisdom and promises. When Habakkuk received the revenue of responses that God freely gave, he concluded his short journal with a song that could not be stopped. The melody bubbled up inside of Habakkuk although his circumstances had not changed.

What *had* changed was Habakkuk's perspective because he now viewed life through the lens of the Father. Habakkuk had heard from heaven and had grasped the answers that God had provided.

Habakkuk broke out in a song that deserves to be remembered today.

There Is Something About a Song

The lyrics of Habakkuk's song echo through the years and call us to a place of heartfelt worship in spite of our circumstances.

Though the fig tree should not blossom and there be no fruit on the vines, though the yield of the olive should fail and the fields produce no food, though the flock should be cut off from the fold and there be no cattle in the stalls, yet I will exalt in the LORD, I will rejoice in the God of my salvation. The Lord GOD is my strength, and He has made my feet like hinds' feet, and makes me walk on my high places. —Habakkuk 3:17–19

If these words had been written during the twenty-first century, perhaps Habakkuk would have exclaimed:

Though the stock market should fail and though I should lose my job, though my house is in foreclosure and I lose my cars, though I am forced to get food from the food pantry, and though I am unable to provide Christmas presents for my family, yet I will exalt in the Lord, I will rejoice in the God of my salvation! The Lord God is my strength and He has raised me above my circumstances. He is all I need!

Habakkuk is coaching all of God's people in all of the epochs yet to follow that the best time to praise the Lord is when you have had the very worst week of your life. If you are walking through a fierce storm or a raging fire, start singing and don't stop. Do not allow disappointment or discouragement to squelch your song of praise to the Father.

There is something about a song that will water the dry and barren ground of your life in a miraculous and monumental way. There is something about a rich, deep melody that will hold thoughts of doubt and anger at bay. There is something about the choice to worship, especially when your world is falling apart, that will renew your hope and guide your heart to health. There is just something about a song!

It's Not a Solo

Habakkuk is not the only person in the Bible who defaulted to a hymn when life had been devastating. David—the king, psalmist, and giant slayer—also chose to belt out an unstoppable melody in the middle of difficulties.

David was desperately trying to escape from the evil intent of Saul and was caught in the middle of a fierce conflict with King Achish when he wrote these lines and set them to a tune of his own making:

I will bless the LORD *at all times; His praise shall continually be in my mouth. My soul will make its boast in the* LORD; *the humble will hear it and rejoice. O magnify the* LORD *with me, and let us exalt His name together.* —Psalm 34:1–3

David knew what you and I often ignore—that every day is a great day to praise the Lord. He refused to be tormented by the battle but chose instead to worship in the face of the battle. David was more aware of the Lord's presence than he was of the presence of the enemy.

When your life is imploding around you, lift your hands in the air and declare with David, "*I will bless the* LORD *at all times; His praise shall continually be in my mouth.*"

Genuine worship does not happen when life is easy and when the blessings are flowing around you. Heartfelt and sincere worship is always birthed in the adversity of life. True praise is conceived in the face of struggles and in spite of constant adversity. The richest melody of your life will sing above the storm and will drown out the roar of the fire. The most vibrant song will be heard with tears rolling down your cheeks and your heart quaking in fear.

Can't Let It Go

As I write these words on this dark autumn afternoon, my heart is unable to let go of the underlying certainty of Habakkuk's song. Oh, that I would have the tenacity of Habakkuk and choose to sing even when I don't like what I see in the natural. Oh, that I would attach the melody of my life to the promises and wisdom of my loving Father. Oh, that the ravages of life lived this side of eternity would never again have the deceptive power of causing me to whine rather than to worship.

There is no more vital issue that will determine your ability to live a vibrant life than your choice to sing. I can't sing for you; you must sing for yourself. However, I can *dare* you to sing—and I do! I dare you to burst into a song of joy regardless of what you are walking through today. The world around you needs the hope that only your song can bring, so sing it. I dare you!

What if the current difficulty that you are experiencing was given to you as a platform upon which to sing the most triumphant song of your life? What if the trial that assails you today is the stage upon which the world will listen to your song? What if…?

When you choose to serenade the Lord rather than worship your circumstances, a miracle happens. You will become someone you never could have been without the defiant song of your life. The atmosphere of your life will miraculously change in an instant with the undeniable gift of your melody.

Though the cherry trees don't blossom and the strawberries don't ripen, though the apples are worm-eaten and the wheat fields stunted, though the sheep pens are sheepless and the cattle barns empty, I'm singing joyful praise to GOD. *I'm turning cartwheels of joy to my Savior God. Counting on* GOD's *Rule to prevail, I take*

heart and gain strength. I run like a deer. I feel like I'm king of the
mountain! —Habakkuk 3:17–19 MSG

I pray that the song of Habakkuk will fill your heart and your mouth today. I pray that the theme of your life will be one of worship and not of discontent. I pray with Habakkuk and with David that this verse will be the theme of your life:

And my tongue shall declare Your righteousness and Your praise
all day long. —Psalm 35:28

Would you pray with me today:

Lord, I declare this day that I will sing in the storm! I will sing during sorrow. I will praise Your name at all times. Father God, Your praise will continually be in my mouth. I worship You, my Savior and my Friend! In Jesus's merciful name I pray. Amen.

No words can express how much the world owes to sorrow.
Most of the Psalms were born in a wilderness. Most of the
Epistles were written in prison. The greatest thoughts of the
greatest thinkers have all passed through fire. The greatest
poets have "learned in suffering what they taught in song."
In bonds Bunyan lived the allegory that he afterwards wrote,
and we may thank Bedford Jail for The Pilgrim's Progress.
Take comfort, afflicted Christian! When God is about to
make preeminent use of a person, He puts them in the fire.
—George MacDonald

13

Who Wouldn't Want That?!

The ability of God to turn bad into good, pain into joy, deserts into gardens, and a wilderness into something bountiful is a theme in Scripture that cannot be overstated. We must remember that what we view as horrific from an earthly point of view is often the fodder from which God creates our very destiny and purpose. What we forlornly suppose is the worst time of our lives, God is able to revolutionize into a springboard of ministry and a riverbed of divine appointments. God is able to turn the charred remnant of our lives into something of spectacular beauty. What we believe is devastating beyond belief, God is able to transform into a stunning miracle. That's the power and creativity of the God we serve!

Something New

Do not call to mind the former things, or ponder things of the past. Behold, I will do something new, now it will spring forth; will you

not be aware of it? I will even make a roadway in the wilderness,
rivers in the desert.   —Isaiah 43:18–19

If you long for the Lord to do something new in your life, there is a prerequisite that must take place. You must leave the past where it belongs before He is able to do a new work in you and for you. If you can discipline your mind not to dwell on past sins, haunting regrets, and sordid disappointments, you will find that the Lord miraculously sets you into a new destiny and fresh opportunities.

You must remember, however, to fulfill your part of this pioneer investment. Many people wallpaper their minds with regrets and their hearts with the happenings of yesterday. These comatose folks will never move beyond yesterday and they refuse the advancement that the Father has for them.

What is it that holds you back from this brand new, one-of-a-kind life that the Father has created for you? It's you! *You* hold yourself in hostage when the anguish of yesterday and the nostalgia of your history become more important than what lies ahead.

I have heard it said that the reason a vehicle's rearview mirror is so much smaller than the windshield is because it is more important to see what is ahead than what is behind. So it is in life, my friend. The view ahead of you is so much more majestic and fascinating than anything in the wake of your life.

Many people foolishly think that they are able to walk backwards through life and still live a life of valor and ambition ... but nothing could be further from the truth.

If you insist on walking backwards with your eyes fixed firmly on the past as you go through life, you will stumble on things that otherwise would not cause you to trip. You will also have an incredibly difficult time reaching your destiny if you stubbornly refuse to turn around and look toward your future.

The brilliant scholar and theologian C. S. Lewis reminds us of this biblical truth with these words: *"There are far, far better things ahead than any we leave behind."*

A Way-Maker

God has guaranteed that He is a Way-Maker and He can make a road in the most parched season of your life. He can use your wilderness as a potent springboard to advance you right into your next assignment. Your wilderness is never wasted when you partner with God on your life's journey.

Your wilderness has the potential to become the most purposeful and productive place that you have ever visited. How does this happen? It happens when you refuse to drag the problems of the past or the memories of yesterday into the glory that is today. If you can effectively abandon the issues that constituted your history, the Lord will work a miracle in the dry places of your life. Isn't that simply amazing?!

The Lord never meant for the wilderness to imprison you or for your past to paralyze you. The archives of your life were meant to be the starting gate for ministry, for compassion, and for hope. Even a wilderness experience becomes a place of rich growth when you choose to partner with Him rather than with your discouragement. I can assure you that in the barren places of life, God is with you just as He is when life is full and fruitful.

In the midst of the dry, barren wasteland that threatens to dehydrate your heart, you will see a rushing river spring up! The Source of the river is Him and He splashes His joy and life onto every grain of sand, every dry crevice, and every wasted bush. *Who wouldn't want that?*

Beauty only grows when it is near a perpetual source of water; vegetation only thrives when it is planted adjacent to an active water supply. You, my friend, will only flourish in direct relationship to your nearness to a fount of Living Water. All of our refreshing comes from the Lord. In Him are springs that never will run dry. He is the birthplace of rivers and streams that will never cease to flow even during times of deep pain. He is your Sustenance, your Source, and your Joy.

The Worst Becomes the Best

One of the most famous pieces of literature ever written, *A Tale of Two Cities* by the iconic Charles Dickens, begins with these words, "It was the best of times, it was the worst of times." This incomparable author recognized a fact that you and I might sometimes ignore: two extremes are able to coexist or occur at the same moment. Radical opposites are not mutually exclusive. Just ask Isaiah.

To grant those who mourn in Zion, giving them a garland instead of ashes, the oil of gladness instead of mourning, the mantle of praise instead of a spirit of fainting. So they will be called oaks of righteousness, the planting of the LORD, that He may be glorified.

—Isaiah 61:3

How wonderful to know that we are able to participate in what I like to call *the great exchange*! Regardless of how deep your mourning has been and how expansive it has grown, the Father offers you a garland in place of the ashes of death. It is not necessary for you to live as a person whose life has been ravaged by pain and sorrow because you are chosen and not forsaken. In the middle of human disappointment, you are invited to live as royalty. You are bedecked as one who is ready for a grand celebration rather than one who is on the way to a funeral procession. You are not singing the dirge of the mourners, but you are shouting songs of joy! You are not slogging through life with your head bowed low, but you are dancing because of the One who has called you and knows you.

Even your identity has changed due to this grand exchange that has taken place when you exchange *"all that I am for all that He is."* Your name can no longer be Weak, Fragile, or Unseen; you are now known as an *Oak of Righteousness*.

An oak tree is a solid and nearly immovable tree due to the unseen depths of its root system. Even when the high winds of storms assail a massive oak tree, limbs might fly off and leaves might be removed, but the tree itself remains stable and firm. You are like that substantial oak tree that the prophet Isaiah mentions; it is His righteousness that gives you your stability. *Who wouldn't want that?!*

Would you pray with me today:

Lord Jesus, today I declare that I will put the past in the past and that I will leave it there. I thank You, Jesus, that You are my Way-Maker and that even today, You are making a beautiful way for me. I am delighted to do the great exchange with You and I accept Your garland, the oil of gladness, and the mantle of praise. In Jesus's powerful name I pray. Amen.

Many men owe the grandeur of their lives to
their tremendous difficulties.
—C. H. Spurgeon

PART FOUR

"Whatever!"

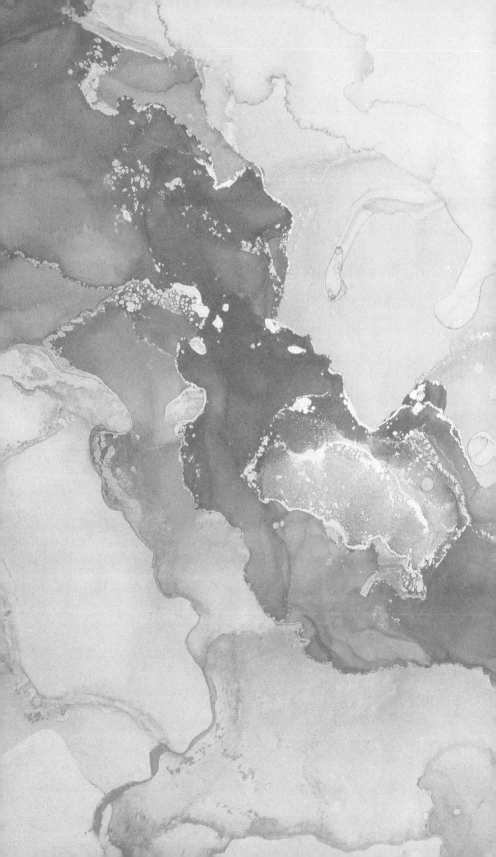

14

Chosen

As a child, I was very close to my Aunt Marianne, affectionately known as "Auntie," and her dear husband, Uncle Doug, who were public school teachers. They loved the children of others for many years before they finally established their family through adoption. I'll never forget the remarkable day when Joy, my sweet cousin who is six years younger than I am, was delivered to our family. The entire family was completely giddy over the fact that we were about to add a darling baby girl to the family tree. My mom informed me early one May morning that she would arrive that historic day, so I spent the entire day sitting on the lamppost in front of my family home. I watched every car that went by with my eager six-year-old eyes and refused to go inside even to eat my lunch. My mother brought me a tuna sandwich, chips, and a glass of milk while I was waiting for my new cousin.

When I finally saw Auntie and Uncle Doug's car drive slowly past our driveway, they honked at me and I ran across the country road and around the corner to meet them on their front porch. Oh, what a thrill it was to cuddle that little chosen baby girl! Although she had not grown inside my aunt's womb, she had grown in all of our hearts for many months.

After Joy was adopted, Auntie and Uncle Doug also added Paul and Anne through the miracle of adoption and their family was then complete. As their children became old enough to understand the circumstances of their births, my aunt and uncle would read to them a cherished book about being *chosen.*

I remember thinking, as a young girl only eight or ten years old, *I wish I had been a chosen child.* I believed that being *chosen* was so much more exciting than simply being born.

Most Valuable

If I were asked to teach on the most valuable verses in the Bible for women, the passage that we are about to linger over would certainly be in contention for that prestigious spot. These six verses, from the book of Colossians, are vital for you, as a child of God, to embrace the delight of walking in your destiny in Christ. They have the potential to revolutionize the legacy that you will certainly leave your family. This sextuplet of verses, written by the hand of Paul under the unction of the Holy Spirit, have the exciting capacity to enable you to *outlive* your life. I believe they will coach you to live as a victorious Christian regardless of the circumstances surrounding your existence.

Let's read this portion of Scripture in its entirety and then we will chew on it, phrase by wonderful phrase, in the next few chapters.

---

*So, as those who have been **chosen by God**, holy and beloved, put on a heart of compassion, kindness, humility, gentleness and patience; bearing with one another, and forgiving each other, whoever has a complaint against anyone; just as the Lord forgave you, so also should you. Beyond all these things, put on love, which is the perfect bond of unity. Let the peace of Christ rule in your hearts, to which indeed you were called in one body; and be thankful. Let the word of Christ richly dwell within you, with all wisdom,* *teaching and admonishing one another with psalms and hymns and spiritual songs, singing with thankfulness in your hearts to God. Whatever you do in word or deed, do all in the name of the Lord Jesus, giving thanks through Him to God the Father.*

—Colossians 3:12–17

Heart's Desire

I believe that deeply nestled inside of a woman's tender heart is the sweet desire to simply be chosen by someone. In the third grade, we long to be chosen for the kickball team. In the fifth grade, we long to be chosen to be someone's best friend. In high school, how we long to be chosen as someone's prom date! As we grow older, we long to be chosen for other things, such as a scholarship, a job, or marriage.

Regardless of who else has rejected you, oh woman of God, rest assured that you have been chosen by the One who loves you most and knows you best! God has chosen you as His very own daughter and intimate friend.

"So, as those who have been chosen of God…." These stirring and dearly comforting words begin this dynamic portion of Scripture. Allow those words to tarry in your love-starved soul. Perhaps you would even consider saying it out loud right now as you are reading these words, *"I have been chosen by God!"*

The Father has chosen you specifically at this time in history to be on His team and to be embraced by His love. He has chosen you to dance through life with Him; He has chosen you to be the object of His blessing and favor. You, my friend, have been chosen by the One who matters the very most.

Knowing that you have been chosen by the Father changes everything for you. It transforms your identity and magnifies your purpose. Every morning when you awake, the first thought that crosses your foggy brain should be, *I have been chosen by the Father!* As you stumble to the bathroom to brush your teeth, the first audible expression that passes those pearly whites should be, *"I have been chosen by the Father!"*

When a person is chosen for a job, for a scholarship, or as a life's partner, it reveals the opinion of the one who has made the selection. God looked out across the sands of time and His gaze focused on you. You were the one that He wanted to spend time with and partner with in loving a lost world back to health. You were the one whom He deemed as a perfect fit for His love and His glory. God's opinion of you is that your very presence brings joy to the Father's heart. He wants you to belong to Him!

The word *chosen* in this verse is the Greek word *elektos*, which some may translate as "elected." This word, however, comes from two Greek words: *ek*, which means "out," and *lego*, which is translated "I say."[3] As you can see, when we combine these words into one meaningful phrase, *elektos* literally means, "Out, I say!"

Allow your mind to wander back to the moment that you found Christ. His voice was shouting across eternity and His eyes were on you. The Holy Spirit had been on a desperate rescue mission to find you so that you could discover Him, the One who also created you. When the Father knew that you had turned toward Him, His voice became a roar of compassion and purpose as He shouted loud enough for all of the demons of darkness to hear, "Out, I say!"

He wanted you for His very own and so He chose you before the beginning of time.

Naming Rights

Not only did the Father choose you, but He also named you. Your past doesn't have the right to name you, nor do your failures have the power to identify you. The only one who holds your naming rights is the One who loves you enough to choose you for His very own.

Paul wrote his letter to the church at Colossae when he was imprisoned in Rome. Even in prison, Paul was thinking about the Father's great love for His children. Paul wasn't content to be mired in discontent or to be

3. Rick Renner, *Sparkling Gems from the Greek, Volume 2* (Tulsa, OK: Harrison House, 2016), 427.

paralyzed by blame, but he used his time in prison to encourage the saints at Colossae and therefore us as well.

After Paul stated that you have been strategically chosen, then he revealed what the Father's choice of name was for those that He had selected. You have been identified as *"holy"* and *"beloved."* Just as people are identified by a first name and a last name, heaven has given you two names as well.

Animals and plants are always identified by two distinct scientific names: genus and species. Your genus is *"holy"* and your species is *"beloved."* *How wonderful is that?!*

Exclusively His

The word *holy* has several different definitions and we will spend sweet time together as we traipse through each one. We will wring the truth out of this remarkable word until we accept it as our very identity.

At first glance, the initial meaning of the word *holy* is a bit challenging, but as you read this definition, don't be discouraged. This word is too glorious to allow discouragement to keep us at arm's length from its impact.

Holy can be translated to mean "things on which account of some connection to God possess a certain distinction and claim." Paul is reminding God's people that because of your direct connection to God, you also possess a certain distinction. Not only are you chosen, but you are a person of eternal distinction!

The second meaning for *holy* is immediately exciting: "something that is so hallowed that you would consider it to be very precious."

Now we know that you are chosen, you are distinct, and you are precious! The list of amazing characteristics that you possess continues to grow. Remember, we are evaluating God's opinion concerning your identity. He has spent eternity past thinking about your individual life and His heartfelt opinion is that you are precious.

Another amazing definition for the word *holy* is "persons whose services God employs." You got the job! God needed someone just like you to serve His kingdom today and as He looked over the world that He had created, His eyes stopped on you. He has purpose for you today.

And finally, the remaining definition of the word *holy* is "set apart for God, exclusively His." You belong exclusively to your Father and He is not very good at sharing. As you travel through the expanse known as life, let me challenge you to live a life that is exclusively given to God's plans and purposes. Don't waste your time flirting with the world for even one valuable minute. Don't throw one day away being spiteful or controlling. Instead, allow your life to be a glorious demonstration of His holiness!

My friend, holiness is not about what you look like on the outside, what you wear, how you speak, or even where you choose to attend church. Holiness is not about what you do, but it is all about who you are. Holiness happens in a woman's life when her daily choices and personal preferences flow out of her God-given identity. My actions are marked and my tongue is controlled because I have been chosen by Him.

Because the Father chose me, I choose differently.

Beloved

How I love this word *"beloved"* in its original form in the Greek! It is a dear word filled with tenderness that was created to convince God's children that we will love being loved by the Father. There is no greater earthly joy than to bask in the truth that we are His beloved.

First of all, the word that is translated as *beloved* is the Greek word *agapao*. As you might have guessed, this comes from the Greek word *agape*. The form of *agape* that is used in this verse is of great significance because of the tense that is utilized. *Agapao* communicates the immutable fact that God has loved us in eternity past, He still loves us today in the present, and He will always continue to love us in the future.[4]

God's love is not conditional upon your behavior; it is the essence of His character. You are unable to obstruct God's love for you, to minimize His love for you, or to choke out His love for you.

---

4. Renner, *Sparkling Gems from the Greek, Volume 2*, 428.

In its most expansive definition, *agapao* can mean "to welcome, to love dearly." You are welcomed into God's family with no reservations and no regrets. What wonderful news! The welcome mat to God's presence is always out for you.

This touching Greek word also means "to have a preference for someone and to wish well." God, in all of His glory, prefers you and deeply desires for you to live a life of emotional health and splendid purpose.

We must not finish our study on the word *agapao* until we digest its final and perhaps most significant meaning: "being willing to suffer for the other person's well-being." Jesus loved you so dearly and so thoroughly that He was willing to die in your stead.

You are chosen. You are holy. You are dearly loved.

Would you pray with me today:

Father, I thank You today that I am chosen, I am holy, and I am completely loved by You. I give You my life today and ask You to use me however You wish. I am Yours, Lord. Everything I have, everything I am, and everything that I hope to be is completely Yours. In Jesus's captivating name I pray. Amen.

⌁

I am His by purchase and I am His by conquest; I am His by donation and I am His by election; I am His by covenant and I am His by marriage; I am wholly His; I am peculiarly His; I am universally His; I am eternally His.
—Thomas Brooks

15

It's All About the Clothes

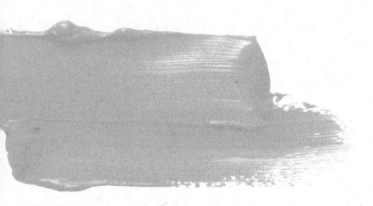

As women, we know the importance of dressing appropriately for the occasion and the weather. We would never wear running shoes to a formal event, or a skimpy tank top outside on the snowiest day of the year. Every woman knows that you must take into account the climate, the event, and the expected propriety in selecting your wardrobe.

Once a woman determines the type of clothes that a given day or a particular event requires, she then probably looks at what she has in her closet to make a final selection. My *eyes* simply have the ability to peruse what is in my closet, but my *hands* must reach in there, take the clothes off the hanger, and then put the clothes on my body. I have never known my clothes to jump off the hanger and onto my body without my help! I must choose to put them on physically, not just mentally.

Now, let me give a little bit of instruction concerning this chapter so you don't become weary or frustrated. Have you ever been looking for *the perfect outfit* to wear and it has taken you literally hours—even days—of shopping in order to find it? Well, this chapter is a long one, but remember, you are on the hunt for a perfect life of unequaled vibrancy. So, take your time as you read this chapter and enjoy every minute of the hunt.

Be a "Put-On"

After the Holy Spirit, through the pen of Paul, fully informs us of our selection by Christ and of His opinion concerning our value, He then explains the practical assignment that is now ours.

Put on a heart of compassion, kindness, humility, gentleness and patience.   —Colossians 3:12

The Holy Spirit has chosen a wardrobe that is specific for your life. It works in every emotional climate, it will protect you in every storm in life, it never goes out of style, and it is always appropriate. However, you must decide to put it on. The Holy Spirit has placed it in your spiritual closet, but you are the one who must choose it day after day.

Merely thinking about this wardrobe will do you no good at all; you must determine to put it on. Simply reading your Bible and looking at these vital wardrobe components will not change your life; you must put them on. It will take an obvious act of your will. When you want to dress in your pre-Christ wardrobe, you will find that it doesn't fit well and that it draws attention to self and not to Christ.

When you choose to put on impatience rather than compassion, you will discover that you are not prepared for the storms in life. When you choose to exhibit pride rather than humility, your life might come apart at the seams. When you choose to be verbally cruel rather than kind, you will find yourself exposed and embarrassed.

Will you choose your pre-Christ wardrobe, or the one that the Holy Spirit has offered to you? I can't choose for you; you must choose your own emotional and spiritual clothing for every day. It's up to you.

Compassion

Compassion is the deepest type of mercy that a human being can experience. The challenging aspect of this wardrobe component is that many people pretend to be compassionate, but pretense just doesn't work. You can't pretend to have compassion; you must *be* compassionate.

Choosing to wear compassion implies opening your heart and allowing the love that resides there to flow toward people. The compassion that you exhibit will make a profound difference in someone else's life.

When [Jesus] *went ashore, He saw a large crowd, and felt compassion for them and healed their sick.* —Matthew 14:14

I have found in my life that it is easy to feel compassionate toward starving children in Africa and thereby send a donation in my stead. It is simple for me to give to a media fundraiser that helps a hospital or a homeless shelter. Our family has even adopted several children over the years who live in Third World countries and we dutifully send our monthly support.

However, I must willingly put on compassion in my home daily; I must assertively choose to put on compassion with the difficult people who surround my life. I have often had to repent for being less than compassionate with the people who live in my very own home!

I have learned, much to my chagrin, that hard-hearted attitudes do not make a difference in the lives of people I know, but compassion *does* make a difference. I woefully admit that judging and criticizing doesn't change anyone's life, but compassion is able to stir up the birth of change for the better.

Everyone realizes that yelling, demanding, or pouting are not compassionate ways to deal with people. However, merely choosing not to be unkind is only the beginning. After identifying what character traits are not compassionate, then you must put on those virtues that exhibit compassion.

Compassion Works

One cold, blustery day years ago, my three younger children and I were making a quick stop at the mall on a Friday afternoon. Jordan, at age seven, was a marvelous helper with his two little sisters, Joy, then four, and Joni Rebecca, then just under a year old. As I was placing Joni in her stroller, I instructed Joy to hold Jordan's hand. We were rushing across the parking lot when I saw a young mother, her two young children, and a middle-aged woman whom I presumed to be the mother of the younger woman. The toddler in the stroller was angry and crying and was in the throes of what I would label a full-blown temper tantrum. The little family had stopped beside a car as the inexperienced mother tried to deal with her out-of-control child. The grandmother held the hand of the other child, who was watching all wide-eyed. The desperate mother began yelling at her child and then unbelievably put her hands around that child's neck. I said a quick prayer because I knew that I had to step in.

I told Jordan to stand between two parked cars with his little sisters and not to move at all. I quickly walked over to the distraught family and quietly said, "You know, I am the mother of five children and I have learned that anger never works."

The grandmother viewed me through guarded eyes while the mother seemed horrified that I had observed that scene.

"I read a book that changed the way that I parented," I continued. "The name of the book is 'The Strong-Willed Child' by Dr. James Dobson[5] and I know that there is a bookstore in the mall that carries the book. I would highly recommend it."

The mother never spoke a word to me but the grandmother said, "Thank you. I will make sure that we get it."

I walked away from that unforgettable scene, not sure if I had made a long-term difference or not, but grateful that God had given me words of compassion in a difficult situation. Honestly, what I wanted to do was scream at the mother that she had no business parenting children. My heart

---

5. Dr. James Dobson, *The New Strong-Willed Child: Surviving Birth through Adolescence* (Carol Stream, IL: Tyndale House Publishers, 2004).

was in my throat and my adrenaline was roaring; however, it was prayer that caught me by the heart and helped my response to be compassionate.

My children and I continued into the mall while I explained to them that we would have lunch and then pray for that dear family. After feasting on chicken sandwiches and fries, my children and I made our way down to the Christian bookstore to do a little shopping. As I was walking down the aisles, I saw the grandmother. She looked at me and said, "I thought you were an angel in the parking lot! My daughter won't listen to me and I have been at my wit's end. Could you please tell me the name of that book again?"

I showed her that particular book by Dr. Dobson as well as a couple of other books that had helped me in my parenting journey. I also purchased two books for preschool children, which I gave to the grateful grandmother.

I have prayed often for that family over the years and have been so honored that the Lord gave me a garment of compassion to wear that day.

Kindness

The second valuable component in your wardrobe is the garment of kindness. Kindness is classic and never goes out of style! Kindness includes a willingness to serve others and make a personal readjustment in order to do so. A truly kind person is adaptable or compliant to the needs of others. Kindness is a virtue that is in direct opposition to the lifestyle that the world encourages us to embrace—one of self-advancement, self-centered decisions, self-pride, and self-esteem. The Word of God calls us, as the children of God, to live a lifestyle of adaptability rather than control.

The Bible reminds us in 1 Corinthians 13:4 that *"love is kind."* Therefore, if we truly love someone, we will make sure that kindness leads the way in conversations and in actions. I have often wondered if kindness is a litmus test that demonstrates the depth of my love for an individual.

As you daily decide to add kindness to your wardrobe, you will surprisingly find yourself asking questions like this:

+ Is there anything that I can do to serve you today?

+ Is there anything that I can do for you that would make your life easier?

+ Can I change my schedule or my expectations in order to accommodate you?

Some people are naturally kind and it is a resource of their temperament while others have to work more diligently at it. For those of you who have to remind yourself to put on kindness above everything else, perhaps it would be important to recall that kindness is a fruit of the Holy Spirit. If your kindness is at an all-time low, the first step that you should take is to dig more deeply in your relationship with the Father. When you spend time with the Lord, you become more like Him and He will rub off on you! The kindness of the Father is a visible theme throughout the central book of Psalms; when we cultivate an intimate relationship with Him, we begin to mirror His character.

One of the primary places where kindness should be most obvious is in the words that we speak and the manner in which we speak our chosen words.

The teaching of kindness is on her tongue. —Proverbs 31:26

The *"excellent wife"* referenced in Proverbs 31 had made it a practice or a habit to only speak words of kindness. How I long to be that kind of person! How I deeply desire to be someone who is characterized by the asset of simple kindness. The legacy of kindness should be something that we all aspire to leave in our wake regardless of our marital status, our socioeconomic level, or our education. Leaving a legacy of kindness should be one of the highest goals in the life of a man or a woman. Rather than being remembered for the money you made, the mountains you climbed, the boards you served on, or the promotions you earned, the most lasting legacy will *always* be one of kindness. Always.

Do you think lightly of the riches of His kindness and tolerance and patience, not knowing that the kindness of God leads you to repentance? —Romans 2:4

If God, in His infinite wisdom, has determined that kindness will turn someone's heart toward repentance, I believe we should wholeheartedly follow His divine example. What works for the Father will certainly work for us. I must remind myself time after time that I don't have a better idea than God; therefore, I will be a woman whose very life is built upon the foundation of sincere kindness.

Do not let kindness and truth leave you; bind them around your neck, write them on the tablet of your heart.　　—Proverbs 3:3

It costs nothing to be kind and yet it is the most extravagant gift you could ever give.

Kindness Looks Good on You!

After three boisterous and lively boys, Craig and I were blessed with a darling little girl who we named Joy, followed nearly four years later by another beribboned bundle who was named Joni Rebecca after both of her grandmothers.

The church family that we pastored at the time had watched Craig and I parent our three sons with patience and resolve as we dealt with loud voices, imaginary boxing matches, and running around the church sanctuary after the Sunday service. However, when the two little girls arrived in our home and in our hearts, the church breathed a collective sigh of relief on my behalf.

I quickly came to realize that my precious church family was doting without reserve on my little girls. They showered them with gifts and compliments every single Sunday morning at our little North Carolina church. On the way home from church, it was often necessary for me to do some repair work and bring my daughters' egos down to a manageable size.

As I drove our family's twelve-passenger van toward our Academy Street home, I would look in the review mirror at the little pieces of feminine daintiness in the back seat. My well-known and never worn out phrase to these darling little girls was, "Joy-Belle and Joni Becca, is it more important to be pretty or to be kind?"

"To be kind, mama, to be kind," was Joy's five-year-old response.

Inevitably, I would hear a dear miniature echo coming from the car seat, "I kind, Mama. I kind."

I intensely craved for my daughters to understand that whether they were two years old or twenty-two years old, kindness is a more valuable commodity than outward beauty or the trappings of fashion.

What is desirable in a man is his kindness.   —Proverbs 19:22

The most eternal legacy that we are leaving to those around us is being chosen today. Every day that we are sucking in oxygen, we are storing up memories in the hearts of others who are observing our uncommon lives. As I contemplate what my legacy will be, I hope that if people remember anything about me, it will be that I was kind. One of my sincere goals is to be the kindest person alive at my moment in history. I want people to recall that I was kind when there was absolutely no reason to bestow kindness. I hope that I am not remembered for the money that I made, for the earthly success I achieved, or for the awards that bore my name. I deeply desire that people will remember that I had a kind heart.

How would you like to be remembered? It's an important question to answer. In our quest to have the last word and to speak our version of the truth, we have lost the beautiful life philosophy that it is more important to be kind than it is to be right. The attitude of kindness over opinion must find its resting spot in our marriages, in our parenting, in our relationships with our siblings and parents, in the workplace, in the church, and on social media. I would rather be remembered for my kindness than for my opinions, wouldn't you?

Humility

I believe that kindness and humility are often matching wardrobe pieces, just like a pair of shoes or gloves. Kindness and humility are best experienced when they are worn in tandem.

Humility is the willingness to stoop to any level that is needed in order to be aware of one's littleness. Even as I write that definition, I realize how loudly it scrapes against our twenty-first century mindset. From a secular perspective, humility is often viewed like fingernails on the chalkboard of life.

In ancient times, this word was primarily used to describe servants— and then not in a positive way. However, when the Holy Spirit lassoed this word and used it to describe Jesus and His followers, *humility* became a word of strength and resolve.

Have this attitude in yourselves which was also in Christ Jesus, who, although He existed in the form of God, did not regard equality with God a thing to be grasped, but emptied Himself, taking the form of a bond-servant, and being made in the likeness of men. Being found in appearance as a man, He humbled Himself by becoming obedient to the point of death, even death on a cross.
—Philippians 2:5–8

Those verses, written by the hand of Paul from a Roman prison, challenge me deeply. I am moved with regret as I contemplate the times in my marriage when I have demanded my own way; I hang my head in shame as I recall the moments when I was curt with my mother or demanding with someone who was serving me. The Bible calls me to an attitude of humility; it is not optional apparel, but a vital component of my spiritual wardrobe. I will never live the life that I was created to live until I empty myself of me and fill myself up with Him and all that He is.

I have learned the hard way that a sense of my own weaknesses is healthy, but I must never use my weakness as an excuse that God cannot use me. To do so would be an insult to Him.

The cry of my heart is no longer, "Less of me and more of Him," but it has become the triumphant declaration, "None of me and all of Him!"

Nothing But Humble

Let me quickly assure you that humility is not the same as having low self-esteem or none at all. Humility is an attitude or a life philosophy that lifts others up as more important than oneself. Humility calls kings and queens to a life of service; it requires presidents and world leaders to care more about the needs of others than the comfort of self. Our identity is royalty, but our job description is servanthood.

Humility dares all of us to bow our knees in worship to the One who died so that we could live humbly and reverently.

Do nothing from selfishness or empty conceit, but with humility of mind regard one another as more important than yourselves.

—Philippians 2:3

It is important for me, as a teacher of the Word of God, to ensure that I have presented every concept in a way that is practical. I want you to know beyond any doubt what it means to live a truly humble life each day.

As you ponder the benefits of living a life of sincere humility, perhaps, once again, you might consider asking yourself a series of questions:

- Were my words selfish or unselfish today?
- Did I try to control a situation to my benefit?
- Did I boast about my contributions or successes?
- Did I continually turn the conversation to me?
- Did I often interrupt?
- Did I insist on having the last word?
- Did I listen more than I talked?
- Did I make those with whom I came in contact today feel important?

As you examine your own behavior and heart attitude with those telling questions, you will diagnose your own propensity to be a truly humble person.

Gentleness

In this age of violent movies, turbulent politics, intrusive lyrics, and disturbing reading material, the idea of gentleness might seem archaic or useless. However, I have discovered that gentleness is one of the most potent weapons in my arsenal of faith and of life.

The Greek word for gentleness is *prautes*, which is often translated as "meekness." As we further study this robust word, you will discover that it just may be the strongest and most vibrant attribute that a person is able to possess.

Prautes describes a person who is slow to respond in anger, who is highly patient and has learned to submit his or her will to a higher authority.[6] Therefore, this word does not apply to a weak person, but rather to a person who has learned to control his or her emotional responses in a highly charged situation.

I must admit, I aspire to be a person whose very nature is described by the word *gentle*, but often, I have fallen so short of the virtue of *prautes*.

"Prautes" is found in classical literature to describe a fierce, wild animal that has been tamed from its ruthless, combative instincts. It was also used as a medical term to evidence a soothing medication that is able to calm an angry mind.[7]

As we combine these meanings and usages, what we discover is a gentle person who is able to control herself even in the presence of insults, a person who would never make an angry situation more volatile, but would seek to respond in a placid or amiable manner that creates calm in the midst of chaos.

You will never become the gentle version of yourself through mere self-control; gentleness is always developed as you allow God to control your human nature.

My flesh has been known to rage, rant, and pontificate when I believe that others are wrong. However, the *me* that God wants me to be looks

---

6. Renner, *Sparkling Gems from the Greek, Volume 2*, 694.
7. Ibid.

decidedly different from my righteous indignation. The Holy Spirit calls me to crucify my fleshly opinions and allow myself to be used as a soothing ointment in cantankerous conditions.

When our prayer is, "Lord, use me," He responds with, "Put on gentleness and I will put you to amazing use!"

As I continue to ponder the meaning of the word *gentle* and its practical application to my emotion-driven life, I am reminded that the Lord would never ask me to exhibit a character trait that was not a part of His nature. If I truly want to live a life of incomparable vibrancy, then I know that I must become just like Him.

You have also given me the shield of Your salvation, and Your right hand upholds me; and Your gentleness makes me great.
—Psalm 18:35

A truly gentle person adds strength and greatness to those around her.

Just Stop Fighting!

One of the self-evaluation questions that I have had to ask myself is this, "Carol, are you quarrelsome?" The incriminating truth is that I never instigate a fight ... but I have often had the gall to continue a fight. When I give my husband the silent treatment or corner someone whose political beliefs are different than mine, I am refusing the glorious garment of gentleness.

The Lord's bond-servant must not be quarrelsome, but be kind to all, able to teach, patient when wronged, with gentleness correcting those who are in opposition, if perhaps God may grant them repentance leading to the knowledge of the truth, and they may come to their senses and escape from the snare of the devil, having been held captive by him to do his will. —2 Timothy 2:24–26

When a child of the Father chooses to put on the royal robe of gentleness rather than the tattered rags of a quarrelsome nature, we are able to beat the enemy at his own game! The Holy Spirit, who hasn't changed His opinion in the 2,000 years since the book of Timothy was written, teaches that if you can choose to be gentle, you just might lead someone to repentance. What a wonder! If you will choose gentleness over belligerence, you have the potential of leading someone to truth. If you will choose to be gentle rather than exhibiting a fractious nature, you just might help someone escape from the snare of Satan!

A gentle answer turns away wrath, but a harsh word stirs up anger. —Proverbs 15:1

My little Irish grandmother, who was often known to help the Holy Spirit in His desire to disciple me, used to say, "Carol, you will catch more flies with honey than you will with vinegar!"

I wasn't quite sure what she meant by that sage wisdom when I was just a child, but over the years, I have realized that sweetness is able to diffuse the acidity of anger. Thank you, Gramma!

Patience

*Put on a heart of compassion, kindness, humility, gentleness and **patience**.* —Colossians 3:12

Isn't it interesting that at the conclusion of this expansive list of character traits that the final one is the overcoat of patience? I wonder if the Holy Spirit is saying, perhaps tongue in cheek, *"And when nothing else works, just be patient!"*

Patience is often also translated as "long-suffering." Hmmm … already I don't like the sound of that word and we haven't even begun to study it yet! Long-suffering simply means to suffer long. I understand the "long" part; I just don't want to know anything about the suffering part!

Long-suffering, or patience, is the Greek word *makrothumia* and it's most accurately translated as "the patient restraint of anger, forbearance or long-suffering."

Our flesh bristles at the very thought of being a person who is known for their long-suffering nature. Our flesh wants to immediately spout off everything that it thinks, feels, and believes. However, the nature of Christ within us calls us to something profoundly more merciful than that. We, as children of God, have the nature of God within us. Our Father has been patient with us and so should we be with others.

The Lord is not slow about His promise, as some count slowness, but is patient toward you, not wishing for any to perish but for all to come to repentance.   —2 Peter 3:9

How Christlike it is to be willing to wait a long time for someone to change! You only have two options when you are waiting for someone to change their behavior or their opinions—you can either be frustrated or you can be patient. The length of time that the wait requires will not change; it is *you* who must change. I will choose patience over frustration every time!

There may be some people in your life who are so obnoxious and frustrating that it might seem like retaliation is the only option. However, remind yourself that patience is always the *very best* option. Patience does not mean that you cannot engage in heartfelt and truthful conversations, but your heart attitude must always be one of patience and kindness.

We urge you, brethren, admonish the unruly, encourage the faint-hearted, help the weak, be patient with everyone.
                                    —1 Thessalonians 5:14

Please do not fill your wardrobe with cheap pieces of personality or human preference, but always choose to revert to the smashing wardrobe that the Lord has chosen just for you. While we wait for someone to change, let us be compassionate, kind, humble, and gentle. It is who we are and what we do.

Would you pray with me today:

Lord, more than anything, I want You! I want Your highest and best for my life. Lord, today and every day, I choose to wear compassion, kindness, gentleness, patience, and love. Thank You for providing such a beautiful wardrobe for me to wear! In the name of Jesus I pray. Amen.

All things are possible to him who believes, they are less difficult to him who hopes, they are easier to him who loves, and still more easy to him who practices and perseveres in these three virtues.
—Brother Lawrence

16

Completely Covered

Have you thrown in the towel yet? Are you waving the white flag of surrender? I have come to the sobering realization that in order for me to live a sterling and vital life, I must lay my agenda down and pick up His wonderful agenda. I must stop demanding my own way and submit myself to His higher way. I must acknowledge the well-known fact that I don't have a better idea than God does! I must. I simply must.

As we continue through our journey of these priceless verses in Colossians 3, prepare to be challenged on even a greater level. It's time for each one of us to look at our lives through the perfect mirror of Scripture and determine where our personal makeover needs to begin.

What Would Happen?

Bear with each other and forgive one another if any of you has a grievance against someone. Forgive as the Lord forgave you. And over all these virtues put on love. —Colossians 3:13–14 NIV

There have been epic feuds in human history. Who can forget the angst that existed between the Montagues and Capulets in the great Shakespearean play *Romeo and Juliet*, which ended in the death of the ill-fated lovers? Or the historic duel between Vice President Aaron Burr and Treasury Secretary Alexander Hamilton, which resulted in the latter's death? Or the "war" between the Hatfield and McCoy families over the course of three decades that left twelve dead?

Certainly there needs to be a better way to solve our disagreements, doesn't there? In America, we now use the court system relentlessly to solve everything from parking tickets to murders. Now, don't misunderstand me, I fully believe that in order to keep civil peace in a society, a judicial system is necessary. However, have you noticed that it is not working? There must be a better way! There must!

Paul and the Holy Spirit offer a better way to the church at Colossae in this effective verse written nearly 2,000 years ago. This heaven-birthed advice is still as impressive today as it was then.

These principles from Scripture are tested when there is a grievance or a disagreement between two people. When two individuals, who have been made in the image of God, refuse to agree, what should happen? Should we resort to a duel? Or a feud? Or a civil war?

The words of Paul echo through the millennia and find a home in my heart: *"Bear with each other and forgive one another."*

When It's Too Hard

Corrie ten Boom is one of my heroines of the faith. Corrie and her family lived in Amsterdam and owned a family clock-making business. They were members of the resistance movement and sheltered Jews in their home in the early years of World War II. They called this secret room in their home "the hiding place."

However, they were eventually arrested by the Gestapo. Corrie, her sister Betsie, and their father were all taken to the Ravensbruck concentration camp for the duration of the war. Their cruel captors treated Corrie and Betsie in deplorable ways. Although Betsie died in Ravensbruck, Corrie was released due to a clerical error.

After the war, Corrie returned to Germany and met with two of the inhumane German prison guards who had tortured Betsie. Corrie forgave these people because she refused to live in a prison that others had created.

Corrie's words always linger in my mind when I am tempted to believe that a person doesn't deserve my forgiveness:

Forgiveness is the key that unlocks the door of resentment and the handcuffs of hatred. It is a power that breaks the chains of bitterness and the shackles of selfishness.

I have learned from Corrie's life that we forgive not because the one who caused the pain deserves the forgiveness, but because we don't want to live in a self-made prison. I forgive because I have been forgiven.

Unoffendable

The clarion call of true Christian living is to endure with one another and hold up one another in faith and in prayer. This does not leave room for petty grievances, personal offenses, or disgruntled feelings. What would have happened in human history if men and women had lived by the principles in the Word rather than by the desires of the flesh? What would happen in your marriage if you lived by the principles of the Word rather than by your fleshly offenses? What would happen in your family if the Word of God was honored intently in human relationships?

Please do not allow the least little grievance in a human relationship to rattle you; instead, consider approaching it with grace and fortitude.

One of my most ambitious goals in life is to be an *unoffendable* woman. I simply refuse to be offended. I am not offended by my adult children or their spouses, although not one of us is perfect, nor do we always behave perfectly. My husband, as wonderful as he is, is not perfect either, but I refuse to allow his behavior to offend me. He can burp, watch TV nonstop on a Saturday, forget my mother's birthday, and leave his dirty clothes on the floor, but I will not be offended! I refuse to be offended by the media, by politicians, by preachers, or by my neighbors. I believe that if I choose to be offended, I am giving the other person too much power in my life.

Another ambitious goal that I relentlessly chase after is to raise up a generation of *unoffendable* people.

I have a dream that in eternity, God's history book will include this sentence: "At the first part of the twenty-first century, there was a group of incredible people who refused to be offended, but offered grace continuously!"

Is there someone in your life whom you need to hold up spiritually or emotionally? Is there someone whom the Lord has called you to believe with and for? Currently, I am standing in the faith with a mother over the self-destructive carnage in one of her children's lives. I will not be moved from praying on her behalf. The principle of sowing and reaping is especially apparent as we consider this vibrant way of doing life. If you want someone to bear with you in life, then you better be prepared to bear with them! If you want others to forgive you, then your forgiveness must be given immediately, completely, and fully. You do, indeed, reap what you sow.

Craig and I have been married for forty-three incredible but imperfect years. One of the gold-laced principles that we have come to live by is, "The first one to forgive wins!" What a joy to be able to forgive this man that God has given to me! How wretched it would be if I held every discarded sock, every dirty dish, and every unmet expectation against him.

Craig and I have also learned that when forgiveness is necessary, so is the gift of bestowing an undeserved blessing. In our marriage, forgiveness has only accomplished half of the required healing. When life has been difficult and there have been harsh feelings expressed or bitter words spoken, we quickly forgive, but we also give a blessing beyond the forgiveness. I might make his favorite dinner for him or he might bring me a bouquet of flowers. I might leave him a note on his dashboard or he might make the bed every morning for a week.

What an exquisite way to live! How could we ever imagine that holding grudges and spewing verbal vomit on people could ever be a healthy answer? God's ways are higher and at times harder than our ways, but they are always healthier.

Whoever and Anyone

Oh, Paul! You certainly leave no escape routes when it comes to godly behavior!

Whoever has a complaint against anyone; just as the Lord forgave you, so also should you. —Colossians 3:13

That about covers it, doesn't it? We are called, by the coaching of none other than the Holy Spirit, to forgive whoever has a complaint against anyone. This is called *no-fault* forgiveness. It doesn't matter whose fault it is—it doesn't matter who talked the loudest, yelled the longest, who yelled first, or who forgot the most important issue. Whoever means *you*. You are expected to forgive anyone you might have a complaint against. You are required to live a life of sterling forgiveness and unequaled mercy. What a wonderful life this will be! What a one-in-a-million existence you will live if you submit your life to the authority of the Word of God!

And, if you are audacious enough to argue at this point, Paul gives a simple reminder to those of the faith. The Lord has forgiven us and we can express nothing less than complete forgiveness to others. I was the dysfunctional family member that the Lord forgave. I was the abuser that the Lord chose to forgive. I was the obnoxious one to whom the Lord offered forgiveness. And now, because I have been forgiven, I must once again respond in a Christlike manner.

Forgiveness is the most dynamic choice you will ever make. It will change your life in ways that are powerful and plentiful. Holding onto a grudge will paralyze you and deny you of the life for which you were created. Don't ruin your life with bitter feuding but walk confidently into a life of joy and peace that is guided by forgiveness.

Would you pray with me today:

Lord Jesus, I love You so much. Thank You for Your forgiveness in my life. Help me to forgive others just like You have forgiven me. Help me to forgive the people who have wronged me, mistreated me, mocked me, and gossiped about me. Help me to forgive the people who have been cruel to those I love. I confess today that I am a forgiver. In Jesus's compassionate name I pray. Amen.

⌣

Forgiveness is a strange thing. It can sometimes be easier to forgive our enemies than our friends. It can be hardest of all to forgive people we love.
—Fred Rogers

17

The Finishing Touch

Your shopping spree through the Word of God is not quite complete. He has one final garment in mind for you that will complete your distinctive wardrobe. This is the one piece of spiritual clothing that you should never leave home without and it is vital for making the best impression.

Beyond all these things put on love, which is the perfect bond of unity.   —Colossians 3:14

The Best for Last

Love is that final piece of apparel that will complete your wardrobe as a living, breathing demonstration of Christ. You must wear His love on top of everything else. It is certainly the most obvious piece of clothing that others will see. Love is the garment that brands us as belonging to each other and sharing a kindred purpose and call.

Love is the virtue and the choice that holds all of the other pieces of our wardrobe together as one. Without love, none of the other pieces will fit well; they might even fall off from time to time. However, when we keep our Christian walk held together by love, it offers fullness to life that is undeniable.

Some commentaries equate Paul's injunction to *"put on love"* to the belt that holds everything else in place. Love is the accessory that puts the finishing touch on our wardrobe. However, I like to think of love as our crowning achievement. Love is the crown that should woo the world to our lifestyle and our calling.

There is another portion of Scripture that also proclaims that love is the greatest identifying trait in the life of a believer in Christ.

But now faith, hope, love, abide these three; but the greatest of these is love. —1 Corinthians 13:13

We serve a God who is identified as being Love. Every unfathomable part of God is love and every thought that He thinks is love. Every part of His character is birthed in love and every word that He has ever spoken has been spoken in pure love.

The one who does not love does not know God for God is love.
—1 John 4:8

Love is not just what we do; it is who we are because we belong to the One who is love. Love is not a requirement of behavior, but it is a call to be like the One who created us. Who wouldn't want to be like Him?!

Love should ooze out of our being just like it does the Father's. Love should not only be our chief goal, but it should also be the road upon which we travel.

The following quote is a stirring reminder of the healing and building power of love:

In a world so torn apart by rivalry, anger and hatred, we have the privileged vocation to be living signs of love that can bridge all divisions and heal all wounds.   —Henri Nouwen

The Good, the Bad, and the Ugly

You will never live a vibrant life or an abundant life if you are still struggling with the command to love the people whom God has placed in your life.

Now, let me clearly say that God does not want you to be abused. If you are in an abusive relationship, *leave immediately*. If you are in a relationship with someone who is dealing with an addiction to pornography or drugs, *leave immediately*.

When I encourage you to love people with the love that Christ has placed in you, my oversized umbrella covers difficult people, dysfunctional people, different people, obnoxious people, and unrepentant sinners. However, love is often tough and always calls people higher to Christlike behavior.

The sad truth is that some people are just harder to love than others, aren't they? If you haven't had to stretch your muscle of love in order to love a difficult person, then you don't know what love really is! I remind myself often that *I* was the difficult person who the Father chose to love—and miracle of miracles, He continues to do so! He loves me at my worst and never lets go! He loved me even when I was in my mess and the love continues.

We are called to love others just like He loves us. Will it stretch us? Definitely! Will there be moments we don't feel like loving a challenging person? Absolutely! The undeniable truth is that I often don't feel like loving perfectly lovable people! I only have a human love and so I am desperate for the love of God to grow inside of me.

Love Is Our Theme

If you could ask Jesus anything at all, what would it be? Maybe you would ask Him if He heard your prayers when you prayed. Perhaps you might want to know if you could depend on His promises or not. Let's eavesdrop on a conversation between a scribe and Jesus. This scribe had a very important question to pose to this Man who was also God in the flesh.

During his tenure on earth, Jesus was interrogated by a scribe who presumably worked for one of the religious leaders of the day. These leaders had already conducted their pointed interview with Jesus; they had asked Him the frivolous question of whether it was lawful to pay taxes and then took things to a whole new level by asking about marriage after the resurrection. (See Mark 12:13–27.)

Then a curious scribe—who realized that Jesus had given excellent answers—simply wanted to know what commandment was the most important one of all? Perhaps he was thinking that it was to not commit adultery, to keep the Sabbath day holy, or to not commit murder.

I can imagine Jesus looking into the distance and consulting with His Father on the answer to this probing inquiry. I am sure that it didn't take Him long before He looked back into the eyes of the man who had made religion his life calling and began to quote the words that His Father had spoken to the children of Israel immediately after He had given them the Ten Commandments.

Jesus answered, "The foremost is, 'Hear, O Israel! The Lord our God is one Lord; and you shall love the Lord your God with all your heart, and with all your soul, and with all your mind, and with all your strength.' The second is this, 'You shall love your neighbor as yourself.' There is no other commandment greater than these." —Mark 12:29–31

Christianity begins and ends on our love for God and our love for others. It has always been and it will always be about love. The depth of our love for God is always reflected in the way we treat others. The love that we show to others is birthed out of the love that God has lavishly, unconditionally, and unselfishly showered on us. We are a people who are so filled to overflowing with the love of God that love is the only possible response that we can have. God loves me completely and irrevocably; His love for me is not based upon performance or upon response to Him. Because I am the clay pot that has been caught in a downpour of the love of the Father, I have no choice but to allow that love to splash all over you!

We love, because He first loved us. If someone says, "I love God," and hates his brother, he is a liar; for the one who does not love his brother whom he has seen, cannot love God whom he has not seen. —1 John 4:19–20

God's love in me enables me to love you. When I can't do it on my own strength or with my own will, God is abundantly able to do it through me. When some unnamed person has gotten on my very last nerve and I think that I just might scream … or gossip … or move to Hawaii … or throw something at the anonymous person … I must go back to God and fill myself up with His love so that I am able to love you in spite of me.

The one who says he is in the Light and yet hates his brother is in the darkness until now. The one who loves his brother abides in the Light and there is no cause for stumbling in him. But the one who hates his brother is in the darkness and walks in the darkness, and does not know where he is going because the darkness has blinded his eyes. —1 John 2:9–11

Love is the starting point, the pivot point, and the goal for those of us who choose to walk in the Light of Christ. We can discern whether a man or a woman is walking in the Light of Christ by this one telltale aspect of his or her life. It is not possible to say that we hate someone and declare in the same breath that we love God. You can't have one without the other. Loving people and loving God are undividable.

If you have the nerve to hate a fellow human being—who, like you, has been made in the image of the Father—then you are hanging out in the back alleys of darkness and sin. Come into the light and love somebody!

With hate in your heart, John says, you are sure to lose your way in life. You will be blinded by hate and by sin and will never walk in your destiny in Christ. Your destiny is to love others and to be loved by the Father. Your destiny is to reveal His love to a hurting world in pain.

Don't be fooled by the easy choice of believing that someone is not worth your love, time, or effort. If you think that person is the only one who is impacted by your choice to withhold your love, you are sadly and magnificently wrong, my friend. The hate and the darkness will come back to rob you of your ability to walk confidently into the future that God has for you. You won't go anywhere with hate in your heart! If you harbor animosity, you are sure to live in darkness and quickly stumble and fall. Love will always light your way and will set you in your stellar destiny.

As we continue to study 1 John 2:9–11, you might wonder, *Who is my brother? And am I really his keeper?*

It's a fair question and one that deserves a biblical answer. The word for *brother* that John uses in these verses implies the broader term of *neighbor.* If you are wondering who your neighbor is, it is not simply the people who live next door or on your street. Your neighbor is anyone and everyone in your life!

Bob Goff is an attorney, an ambassador, and an author who takes delight in teaching the world how to love everybody all the time. I had the distinct pleasure of hearing him speak several years ago at a national gathering of young moms. One of the phrases that he used impacted me greatly: *"Start with your most difficult person and love them the most."*

That's quite the challenge, isn't it? *"Start with your most difficult person and love them the most."*

Who is your most difficult person? Is it your boss? Perhaps it is your mother-in-law? Could it be your daughter-in-law—or your very own brother? I hope that it's not your spouse … although it might be! After you have identified your most difficult person, begin today to love that person with an unconditional and vibrant love. Love your most difficult person with a tenacity that never lets go and is never offended. If there is one place in your life where you are allowed to be stubborn, love is the place where stubbornness will cultivate the most vivid results.

You and I were Jesus's difficult people and yet He loved us so much that He chose to die for us! I'm pretty sure that very few of us will be called to die a physical death on behalf of a difficult person. However, I can also assure you that as you choose to stubbornly love the difficult people in your life, you will die to self, die to preference, die to your emotions, and die to your rights. But the glory of it all is that you will live a vibrant and extraordinary life!

Just Admit It

When I decided to write this particular book, it was the deep and aching desire of my heart to coach a generation of Christ-followers how to live a life of extreme purpose, godly principles, and eternal wisdom even while in the humdrum of life. I want you to live fully, exuberantly, and abundantly. The only way that you will ever do this is to attach your life to the principles found in the Word of God.

A large portion of your capacity to live a vibrant life is to love and forgive difficult people. They will be in your life whether you like it or not, so you might as well just go ahead and love them! You can either be frustrated or filled with love; you can either be miserable or filled with love. You can either plot revenge or determine how to love. The choice is up to you. As for me, I'll choose love!

Would you pray with me today:

Lord Jesus, I love You so much. Thank You for Your unconditional, passionate, faithful, enthusiastic love toward me. I love being loved by You. Help me to love the people in my life just like You have loved me. In the loving name of Jesus I pray. Amen.

In the moments right after you die, when you're resurrected "in the twinkling of an eye" and you stand before the sovereign God of the universe, you will fully grasp that this whole world was His, and His purposes were the most important things ever going on in it. And you'll be so unbelievably grateful that you abounded in the work of the Lord with your one and only life. You'll be so glad that you lived full-on for Him.

—Bill Hybels

18

One of Those Days

If you are anything at all like me, there have been many days in your life you could label as *one of those days*. As a woman, a wife, a mother, an employer, a daughter, and a friend, it seems as if someone is *always* expecting something from me that I just can't deliver. In those moments when there is so much confusion, busyness, commotion, entanglements, and people vying for my attention, I just want to scream at the top of my lungs, "Stop the world! I want to get off!"

If you can relate to those frantic moments, perhaps you soothed your nerves by eating chocolate, booking a trip to an exotic location, or spending way too much money shopping. Maybe your idea of escaping the reality of your life is to lose yourself in a ridiculous TV movie or spend hours on social media wishing that you had anyone else's life but your own.

It is on those very days, when the circumstances of life have ganged up on you and bullied you into a mere pulp of yourself, that you need to make a different kind of decision. You need to decide to allow the Word of God to step up into a place of authority in your life! You need to invite the Word of God to step up to the plate in your life and have the last word in you.

Let the peace of Christ rule in your hearts, to which indeed you were called in one body; and be thankful. —Colossians 3:15

How I have always loved the power, the practical application, and the hope that is all packed into this one verse! First of all, allow me to point out that it is written in the imperative; it is not an option for those of us who have faith in Jesus Christ. The Holy Spirit, through Paul, commands believers in all generations to obey in two specific ways:

1. *Let the peace of Christ rule in your hearts.*

2. *Be thankful.*

Paul is talking to *you* in this verse! He has given you some simple pieces of instruction that are going to create a more vibrant and painless life.

Calling the Shots

In the first phrase of this sentence, *"Let the peace of Christ rule in your hearts,"* Paul has utilized sports terminology to make his point. Paul chose to use the word *brabeuo*, which referred to the umpire or referee who made the game-determining calls in athletic competitions. Athletic events were famously celebrated during that era, so the average person knew exactly what Paul was referring to in using this word.

Paul knew that the peace of God needed to call the shots and set the rules in our minds, our will, and our emotions. We should never allow fretfulness, anxiety, or worry to make our decisions. We must allow the peace of God to be in charge in every area of our lives. When we feel overwhelmed by problems or emotions, we simply need to say, "Peace! Take over! I refuse to worry!"

When you are having a hard day and you feel like everything in the world is coming against you, you need to shout, "Peace! Set the boundaries in my life! I refuse to spend one more minute fretting!"

When your relationships are fractious and your resources are at an all-time low, you need to roar, "Peace! Make this call in me!"

Peace will never rule and reign in your heart unless you allow it to do so. When difficult circumstances are attacking your life from every direction, the right choice is to stop for a minute and deliberately set your heart and your mind on the Word of God. When you do this, the victorious peace of God will rise up within you and begin to call the shots. I can tell you from personal experience that it is nothing short of miraculous!

Worry and anxiety are two of the ugliest pieces of clothing in your wardrobe; I have never known a worried person who looked good. Worriers are famous for drawing attention to themselves and their problems. God's wonderful and authoritative peace will call out, "Foul thought!" when a believer begins to worry. Peace cries out, "Trust God!" when anxiety begins to creep in.

But...

You might be thinking at this point in our study of such an applicable verse, *But what is peace? Where is it? And how do I get it?*

Those three questions are all extremely pertinent and must be answered in our quest to fertilize our lives with the truth of Scripture.

The word "peace" comes from the Greek word *eirene*, which communicates the concept of wholeness, completeness, or tranquility in the soul that is unaffected by outward circumstances or pressures. *Eirene* also expresses the thought that if one has embraced peace, it literally defies chaos or trauma. A person who has *eirene* has the ability to behave, think, talk, and emote peacefully even when their entire world is erupting around them. It almost sounds impossible, doesn't it? But I can guarantee you that it is not impossible—in fact, it is *probable* when you know Jesus.

One day, Jesus was having a conversation with His young disciples and He was trying to prepare them for His eventual return to heaven. Can you picture it? As He looked at their faces, tanned by the sun, and their eyes riveted on Him, this is what He said:

Peace I leave with you; My peace I give to you; not as the world gives do I give to you. Do not let your heart be troubled, nor let it be fearful. —John 14:27

What Jesus offers us is always priceless and eternal. The world is not able to grant the peace that the Lord gives. The peace that the world tries to provide is based on circumstances in life. If all is well in our world, then we have some semblance of peace. However, Jesus offers peace in the storm. He gives peace in spite of confusion. He extends peace that surpasses understanding. What a gift!

The steadfast of mind You will keep in perfect peace, because he trusts in You. —Isaiah 26:3

There is only one place to acquire peace and that is at the altar of trust. If you choose not to trust the Lord for the details of your life, peace will always be that elusive butterfly that evades your tentative grasp. However, if you can choose to trust your good, good Father through all of life's mountains and valleys, you will reap the rich harvest of *eirene*.

When I am feeling anxious at the condition of my life, I simply pray, "Jesus, I thank You that You are in control. I trust You to accomplish what concerns me."

And when I pray like that, peace comes rushing in!

And Be Thankful

Oh, how I love the last three words of this verse! *"And be thankful."* What power that tiny trio of words is able to express! The choice to live with a heart overflowing with gratitude just might be the key that unlocks the door to a vibrant, expansive, and beautiful life. It's amazing that such a small decision can unlock such a great door.

When you have chosen to put on compassion, kindness, humility, gentleness, and patience, what is there left to do in order to live a vibrant life?

When you have stood with someone through gale force winds and when you have forgiven and forgiven and forgiven again ... what else is there left to do to live a joyful and abundant life?

When you have put on the overcoat of love and have allowed the peace of God to call the shots in your heart, what else could there be possibly left to do?

The answer is this: just be thankful!

Gratitude in the middle of lack causes a glorious change in one's perspective. Little becomes much when a person simply says, "Thank you."

Enemies become dear friends when a person is bold enough—and humble enough—to say, "I appreciate you."

A heart of gratitude is the very best gift we can ever give to our children. When a mother teaches a child to write thank-you notes, to say thank you in person, and to praise the Lord daily, she is giving her precious child a legacy that will withstand any situation in life.

Did you know that Paul wrote his persuasive letter to the Colossians from prison? Unjustly imprisoned, lacking sufficient food, creature comforts, or proper clothing, Paul professed for all of Christendom to hear, *"And be thankful!"*

I have found that if I am struggling to experience peace, and discontent is knocking at the door of my heart, if I can be thankful for the little things in life, gratitude will grow within me.

I can be thankful for a warm shower, a cup of coffee, and a sweet prayer with my husband. I can give thanks for an encouraging e-mail, the sunshine that creeps in through my windows, and a song that replays on the stereo of my heart. I choose to be grateful for the birds in the tree behind my house, the laughing children who run down my street, and drinking a cup of tea from a fragile cup that used to belong to my grandmother.

As I choose to be thankful, my perspective is sweetened, peace rushes in, and I am content. When I choose to be thankful, it opens my heart and eyes to a grand array of blessings that I had seemed to overlook.

I have heard it said that if you only pray one prayer in life, let it be this one: "Thank You."

Often, when the circumstances of life are excruciating and hope is nowhere to be found, choosing to be thankful is agonizing and seems nearly impossible. In that particular moment, what is needed is a sacrifice of praise.

He who offers a sacrifice of thanksgiving honors Me.
—Psalm 50:23

I am reminded often of the words of the great theologian A. W. Tozer, whose words seem to be imprinted on this heart of mine:

Gratitude is an offering precious in the sight of God, and it is one that the poorest of us can make and be not poorer but richer for having made it.

When you choose to exhibit a heart of gratitude, in spite of your feelings, you suddenly become the very best version of yourself. You become the person who you were made to be at the beginning of time!

Thanksgiving can transform a storm into a time of growth and purpose. Gratitude is able to minimize pain and maximize joy. Every day is a great day that has been given to the wonder of cultivating a thankful heart, a day of grand significance.

Your GPS

Thanksgiving is the most direct and quickest route to living a life of victory. Thankfulness helps you to arrive at the life you have dreamed of in the shortest amount of time possible.

I will admit that I am directionally impaired. North, south, east, and west mean absolutely nothing to me! Even "turn left" or "turn right" is subjective because it depends on which way I am facing. I have learned that

I simply must have my smart phone with me whenever I am in my car in order to get from my house to the grocery store, or to the gym, or to my daughter's house. There are several settings on the particular app that I use, including a setting that states, "Quickest route." I can zip around town and across my state in no time when I have my phone set on that app. I am thrilled that this app can help me to avoid traffic jams, road construction, and accidents.

Setting your heart on the firm discipline of "thanksgiving" is much like my "quickest route" app. You will arrive at your God-selected destiny faster than you could have imagined. Thanksgiving changes your perspective and helps you to navigate through challenging times in life. Doesn't God have the best ideas?

Would you pray with me today:

Lord Jesus, I love You so much. I love everything about You! But today, I am especially grateful for the peace that You have given to me. Thank You for Your consummate kindness, Your unending compassion, and Your spectacular joy! In Jesus's wonderful name I pray. Amen.

⌒

What if, today, we were grateful for everything?
—Charles M. Schulz

19

The Richest Person in the World

*I*t's a *Wonderful Life*[8] has become the consummate Christmas movie. It's the story of an ordinary man, George Bailey, who lives in the small town of Bedford Falls. As a young man, his goal had always been to travel the world, but instead he stayed in the town where he was raised to help sustain the family business. One year at Christmastime, George has a crisis of identity and of faith. After traveling back through time with an angel that the Lord assigned to him, George finally realizes that he is the richest man in the world. He understands that his wealth never came from money or success, but from loving and serving other people.

Perhaps you and I need to reevaluate that which constitutes authentic treasure in our own lives. It might be a valuable self-examination to ask ourselves, "What is it that makes me rich?"

For me, the genuine wealth of my life has always been discovered between the pages of the most powerful book ever written, my Bible.

---

8. *It's a Wonderful Life*, directed by Frank Capra (1946; RKO Radio Pictures).

Don't Laugh!

What is your favorite verse in the Bible? It's a great question, isn't it? Every time I begin a sentence with the words, "This is my favorite verse in the Bible," my friends literally break out into laughter. I have honestly led them to believe that *every* biblical verse is just my *absolute favorite* one.

Now don't laugh like my friends choose to do, but I can assure you that the following verse is certainly in my personal Top 10 List of Bible Verses.

Let the word of Christ richly dwell within you, with all wisdom teaching and admonishing one another with psalms and hymns and spiritual songs, singing with thankfulness in your hearts to God.
—Colossians 3:16

As we chew on this nutritious verse, I believe that you will understand why this book—and actually all of my writing—is so rich in Scripture. The obvious truth is that I have no wisdom or words of instruction from my own human mind. Everything that I am and everything that I have has been fortified by the Word of God. I often declare, "I don't have a better idea than God!"

Richer Than You Think

One of the most consuming *joy-robbers* in my life over the years has been the stress of finances. As the homeschool mother of five children, married to a pastor whose salary was rarely raised, often we had to pray for our next meal or the resources to pay a utility bill. However, early one morning when I was reading my Bible before the children woke up, I discovered that I was richer than I had ever imagined! When my eyes and my heart landed on this magnificent verse, I honestly felt like I had struck a vein of gold so rich and rare that my life would never be the same. I knew that *I knew* the Holy Spirit was speaking directly to my heart as I had an *ah ha! moment* over that which was truly valuable in life.

"*Let the Word of Christ richly dwell within you*" was the advice of Paul to my barren heart. Over the next few days as I studied this phrase, prayed over it, and talked about it with my sweet husband, I realized that I was wealthy in all the ways that actually mattered in life.

The word translated as *"richly"* in this verse is *plousios*, an extremely old Greek word that describes a boundless wealth of which there is no end. Some of the phrases that are used in Bible dictionaries to define this word are so exciting that you just might feel the riches of the ages settle in your spiritual bank account as well:

- Unmatched abundance
- Lavishness beyond expression
- Magnificent affluence
- Riches that have been sought after

I would absolutely love to have those phrases describe the stocks that I own, my retirement fund, or the money in my savings account. However, those words describe something much more important and eternal than earthly finances could ever be.

When I, as a believer in Christ, allow the Word of God to live in the deepest parts of me, all of those terms describe the person that I am! Because of the Bible and its influence in my ordinary life, I am a woman of unmatched abundance. I am a wife who is living a life of lavishness beyond expression. I am a mother who owns riches that others have sought after. I am a daughter whose family affluence is simply magnificent!

Now, before you become too excited, let me remind you how these riches become yours: when you allow the Word of God to go to the deepest places in you. You must invite the Word of God to take up permanent residence in you. Don't treat the Bible like a guest that visits from time to time; instead, establish a foundational place for the Word in your life patterns. Unfortunately, some of us treat the Word of God like an unwanted visitor and we kick it out when it says something with which we disagree.

If you allow the Word of God to build its dwelling place in your heart, you will be the beneficiary of the wisdom, the hope, the joy, and the strength that is required for every day of your life. The Bible is the breath of God that has come to live on the written pages of Scripture. When you open your Bible, you are inhaling the life source of heaven itself. When you read the Words that God has written to His church, you are partaking of divine nourishment that has strengthened men and women of faith in all epochs of human history.

When you take the time to meditate on the truth of the Bible, you are lingering over the divine words that enabled Billy Graham to reach millions for all of eternity. You are ingesting the eternal fruit that sustained Mother Teresa as she ministered to lepers and the poor. When you open your Bible and allow your eyes to roam from page to page, you are reading the words that gave Corrie ten Boom hope in a concentration camp and that spoke to Dietrich Bonhoeffer as he stood against the Nazis.

We all have the same Holy Spirit to give us power and the same Word of God to strengthen us and give us wisdom. We have what the heroes and heroines of our faith had before us. Let's decide today to leave a legacy that causes the generations that will come after us to rise to their feet in a mighty roar!

The Dividends of Your Wealth

The wealth that is yours when you simply treasure the Bible in your heart will bear unmatched dividends in your life.

With all wisdom teaching and admonishing one another with psalms and hymns and spiritual songs, singing with thankfulness in your hearts to God.　　　　　　　—Colossians 3:16

The wisdom of the ages will come out of your mouth as the Word becomes your nourishment. You will be filled to overflowing with the knowledge and discernment of the Lord and it will automatically become part of your speech and how your treat other people. The wisest people in the world do not necessarily have an Ivy League education or a doctoral degree, but they *have* given their life to the study of God's precious Word.

I have more insight than all my teachers, for Your testimonies are
my meditation. —Psalm 119:99

Not only will wisdom become an intrinsic part of your makeup, but you will also have surround-sound joy! The music will never stop inside of you and you will discover that nothing, absolutely nothing, will be able to mute the song that is uniquely yours.

When the Word takes residence in you, so does the symphony of heaven. The Bible doesn't enter into our lives as a solo experience, but it is always accompanied by wisdom and by the eternal hymns of our faith.

Paul reiterates this perpetual call to worship in the letter that he wrote to the church at Ephesus:

Speaking to one another in psalms and hymns and spiritual songs,
singing and making melody with your heart to the Lord; always
giving thanks for all things in the name of our Lord Jesus Christ to
God, even the Father. —Ephesians 5:19–20

Do you see what's hidden in these verses? Paul is coaching us on how to enter a conversation with someone; he is quite pointedly telling us what to say. This is among the most practical Scriptures in the entire New Testament! We are bidden to greet one another with the Word and with songs of joy. We are encouraged to bring valuable phrases of hope and peace to every conversation in which we engage. We need to change the way we talk to one another and about one another! If you long to develop lively and heartwarming relationships with your family and friends, then you should take Paul's advice and speak with God's words.

Perhaps now you might understand why the enemy battles so fiercely to keep believers away from the Word of God. He will try to convince you that you are too busy or that other things should take priority over reading the Bible. The enemy might whisper in your ear, "You can never understand it anyway, so why read it? Isn't it just a waste of time?"

The Word of God goes far beyond being merely informational—it's transformational as well. It will ensure that you have the wisdom you need to parent well and to make godly decisions. The Bible will stabilize your emotions and strengthen you when you are walking through a difficult time. The Word of God will give you a joy unmatched and a zest for life that others will envy.

And more than that, you will be the richest person in the world!

Would you pray with me today:

Lord Jesus, thank You for the Bible. I am amazed at the absolute power that Your Word has in my life. Father, I pray that as I read the Word that You will give me revelation knowledge and that I will hear Your voice speaking to me across the pages. Lord, help me to hide Your Word in my heart. I love loving You and I love reading Your Word. In the wise name of Jesus I pray. Amen.

The more you read the Bible and the more you meditate upon it, the more you will be astonished with it.
—C. H. Spurgeon

20

Whatever You Do and Every Word

Paul and the Holy Spirit have one final piece of advice for us in this memorable portion of Scripture. I wonder if the Holy Spirit said to Paul, "Paul, just in case the believers in the generations to come don't thoroughly understand how to live wholeheartedly and passionately for Christ, let's cover it with one final thought."

Whatever you do in word or deed, do all in the name of the Lord Jesus, giving thanks through Him to God the Father.
—Colossians 3:17

So, my friend, as we close this section of study together, let this verse be your guide throughout all of life. Whatever you do, you should honor the name of the Lord. *Whatever you do!*

Every word that you speak should be wise and kind. Every action that you set your hand to should bring pleasure to the heart of the Father.

At the beginning of every day, give thanks. Every hour of every day should be running over with praise to the Lord and to the Father. And when you lay your head on your pillow at night, as you doze off into a sweet sleep, your last thought of every day should be, "Thanks, Dad. It sure was fun serving You today."

It's Not Too Hard

Now before you throw this book in the trash and scream at no one in particular, "*I can't do that! That is way too hard for me to do all the time,*" allow me to gently remind you that if you have followed the advice of Paul and the Holy Spirit in the previous five verses, you have already done it!

Apply these ten principles to your life daily and you will bring wonderful joy to the Father's heart. The Holy Spirit will stand up and give you a standing ovation as you sweetly serve those around you. Jesus, your elder brother, will high five the Father and cheer, "I knew My friend could do it!"

- Always remember that you are chosen, holy and beloved. Your identity comes from the One who created you.

- Always be compassionate and kind.

- Always be humble, gentle, and patient.

- Hold each other up and always forgive.

- Put on love every day.

- Let the peace of Christ call the shots in your life.

- Be thankful.

- Read your Bible.

- Sing songs of praise without ceasing.

- Whatever you do, make sure that it honors the Lord and give thanks.

Show and Tell

May I just leave you with one more word of advice in this wonderful but challenging section of Scripture?

You can do it! I know you can!

Oh, you might stumble and fall from time to time, but get quickly back on track by reading the Word and by being thankful. The life that is described in these memorable verses from Colossians is the life that the Father has planned for you and it is indeed a wonderful life. You don't want to miss this life!

Anger, shame, criticism, and impatience will never build an astonishing life. The enemy is unable to steal your eternal life from you, so in his sneaky, devious way, he tries to undermine your abundant life. One of the ways in which Satan does this is by convincing you that your feelings matter more than your commitment to the Word. Don't listen to the enemy—listen to God!

When you allow these verses from Colossians to be the compass for your life, you will realize that God has the best ideas of all. You will discover the *you* that you were created to be. And, you will be an earthly show-and-tell of the character of the Father.

Would you pray with me today:

Lord Jesus, I love You so much! I pray that You would overwhelm me with Your power! I pray that You would give me the strength to obey You every day in every way. And Father, I thank You that You are showing me clearly how to make every moment of my life on earth count for all of eternity. In the sweet name of Jesus I pray. Amen.

⌒

The purpose of Christianity is not to avoid difficulty,
but to produce a character adequate to meet it when it comes.
It does not make life easy; rather it tries to
make us great enough for life.
—James L. Christensen

PART FIVE

Walk Worthy

21

He Does It Again

Ιt's difficult for me to imagine the murderer that Paul was before he met Christ on the road to Damascus. Known as Saul prior to that conversion experience, he persecuted the disciples of Jesus and threw them into prison. The Bible recounts the fact that the very reason Paul lived, at one point, was to kill another Christian. The very air that he breathed fueled his hatred against those who believed in the resurrected Christ.

> *Now Saul, still breathing threats and murder against the disciples of the Lord, went to the high priest.*   —Acts 9:1

But this man, formerly the executioner of believers in Christ, had been gloriously changed by faith in Christ and by the indwelling of the Holy Spirit. Paul, who had been born into every advantage and benefit that the Jewish culture could offer, had laid it all aside for the sake of the call of Christ Jesus. Paul wrote thirteen of the twenty-seven books of the New

Testament and is unparalleled in his influence in the lives of believers since the first century.

Paul knew that if *he* could change due to the power of Christ, then anyone could change! Paul's passion for living a life honoring the Lord is vividly expressed in the book of Ephesians. The church at Ephesus was one of the most prominent in early Christendom and Paul visited there often. As a prisoner in Rome, Paul wrote his letter of encouragement specifically to the Ephesians. However, I have always believed that although this letter was written *to* the believers at Ephesus, it was written *for* all of us who choose to live for Christ. So, let's listen in on Paul's advice to this dynamic and thirsty group of believers.

The Persuasive Prisoner

Therefore I, the prisoner of the Lord, implore you to walk in a manner worthy of the calling with which you have been called, with all humility and gentleness, with patience, showing tolerance for one another in love, being diligent to preserve the unity of the Spirit in the bond of peace. —Ephesians 4:1–3

Paul makes a major pronouncement in this verse that is easy to overlook as we slide into his instructions. As I read Paul's declaration, my heart stops its beating and I am forced to evaluate my own life.

"Therefore I, the prisoner of the Lord...."

Paul doesn't recognize that he is being held captive by the Roman government; instead, he clearly states that if he is held hostage by anyone, it is surely the Lord.

As I contemplate Paul's words, I am forced to recognize the fact that we are all *in prison* to something or to someone. There are invisible chains that bind all of us to something in this mortal life. Some people are in bondage to their families, to shopping, to their careers, to entertainment, or to eating. Some are enslaved to politics, to opinion, or to sports. Your prison is the one thing in life that holds you in its vice-like grip. It's a sobering thought, is it not?

So, before we move ahead to the heart of this verse, perhaps we first must acknowledge the prisons that hold us. What prison do you need to be released from? Conversely, in what prison should you be spending time?

In actuality, Paul was in dire need of being released from the Roman prison that held him, but this was not possible with mere human efforts. Paul chose to rise above his human chains and determined to be chained to a more powerful and real prison than any earthly confinement. Paul lived in a prison of absolute freedom!

Paul knew that although the Roman prison might have the power to impede his earthly movement, in being chained to Christ Jesus, he was set free to be the person who he was eternally called to be. Paul experienced more freedom in prison than he had when walking the streets of Rome or Jerusalem. Paul lived for the prison of serving Christ wholeheartedly all the days of his life.

Paul was assured of one overriding blessing from living a Christian life: if you are free in Christ, there is no prison that can hold you back from your destiny!

This is a conundrum, isn't it? What a lovely and hopeful contradiction in terms! My prison frees me to serve Christ with my whole heart.

I hope these words are resonating with those of you who are young mothers or fathers. Although your days may include piles of laundry, disrupted sleep, and nonstop demands, you have the joy of serving with freedom during these years! Sing the Word of God over your children and tell them the stories of Jesus at the breakfast table. When there is chaos in your home, choose to be a man or a woman at glorious peace.

I hope these words are resonating with those of you who are widowed or single. Although your days might be restricted by loneliness and lack of purpose, you have the freedom of serving the Lord with uninterrupted prayer, with hours to volunteer at your church and to invite people into your home. In this season where you have been gifted with excess hours yet denied intimate human companionship, choose to be a person of glorious purpose.

I hope these words are resonating with those of you who are empty nesters or retired. Although your life might be hampered by the call of haunting memories and wondering if you will ever do anything significant again, you now have the freedom to travel, to develop new hobbies, and to mentor others. In this season of transition and loss of purpose, choose to be someone with a glorious identity.

I Beg You!

Paul, a liberated prisoner of the Lord, begged the church at Ephesus *"to walk in a manner worthy of the calling"* with which they had been called. He exhorted them not to settle for mediocrity or a self-centered lifestyle, but to live full throttle in their destiny in Christ Jesus. Paul deeply desired for all of those under his watch to live a great life in heaven's estimation; I believe that Paul's desire not only targeted the church at Ephesus, but also you and me today.

Therefore I, the prisoner of the Lord, implore you to walk in a manner worthy of the calling with which you have been called.

—Ephesians 4:1

If I had been sitting with Paul in that dirty, smelly Roman prison, I would have said with as much respect in my voice as I could muster, "But Paul, what does it mean to walk worthy? Is that even possible for a human to accomplish?"

Of this I am achingly aware: I fail every day in my walk with Christ and as I read these precious words that are stained with tears in my Bible, I humbly confess that I let Jesus down every single day. How can I, as a fallible human being, ever be worthy of my calling in Christ?

But then I hear the sweet whisper of the Holy Spirit remind me, "Carol, this is God's will for your life. Your calling in Christ is to walk worthy and if He called you to it, He will also give you the power to accomplish it!"

Our chief goal this side of heaven should be to live our lives in a way that honors the Father. Paul and the Holy Spirit are pleading with believers to order our days in a way that brings glory to God. We are urged to treat people in such an encouraging manner that it makes the Father's heart happy. Every word that we speak should be a word of kindness and compassion to those in our lives.

We are the Father's representatives on earth and our calling is to represent Him well. We are His ambassadors of hope, joy, and love. People are watching our lives to see Christ in us, the hope of glory.

Paul is such a discerning man that he doesn't leave us hanging with a grandiose statement, but he becomes specific at what it means to walk worthy.

As we continue to dig for gold in the words of Paul, I have a challenge for you. I want you to think of the most difficult person in your life and then I dare you to apply these astonishing principles in the verses that follow to your relationship with that troublesome person. Often it is problematic people who we allow to embezzle our abundant life and then to kidnap the vibrancy for which we were designed.

Would you pray with me today:

Lord Jesus, I just love You so much! I thank You that there is no prison that will hold me back from living a life of freedom and purpose in You! Father, would You help me to walk worthy in Christ? Would You give me the strength and the wisdom that I need to walk in Your truth every day? In the wise name of Jesus I pray. Amen.

I don't know how but I know Who.
—Beth Moore

22

Apply It

Here we go again! We are about to dig into a list of character traits that was written by the hand of Paul under the unction of the Holy Spirit. This time, however, we will apply each trait to the obnoxious, bothersome, and fractious people in our lives. I believe that these verses have the organic power to revolutionize your life as you deal with people you would rather avoid. Paul's input is better than avoidance because his advice comes straight from the throne room of the Father. In all of these challenging relationships, I must finally realize that I don't actually want what I think that I want, but I deeply desire what the Father wants for me.

With all humility and gentleness, with patience, showing tolerance for one another in love. —Ephesians 4:2

Every Saturday morning when my children were at home, they would find their list of chores for the day at the breakfast table. It might include things like:

- Clean under your bed.

- Go through your sock drawer and make sure that each sock has a match.

- Teach your little brother to tie his shoes.

- Straighten the silverware drawer.

- Get all of the trash out of the car.

I wasn't trying to torture my kids with this helpful yet challenging list; I was simply trying to make our lives easier and more fluid. As we read the list that Paul provides, remember that he is not trying to torture you or stretch you beyond what you are able to endure. He is simply trying to enable you to have ease in your formerly demanding relationships.

The Quest for Humility

The call to humility is the call to think modestly or in an unpretentious way about oneself. Humility offers a person no room to embrace a spirit of superiority or to consider oneself as being better than another person. I have had to remind myself numerous times that I am not superior in any way to my most difficult person. I am called, as a woman made in the image of Christ, to honor the person who is challenging for me to love and to whom I must show kindness. Jesus was God in the flesh; He was the King of creation and yet He took on the form of a bond servant. If any one person ever had the option and privilege of thinking highly of Himself, it was Jesus—yet He chose not to do so.

Have this attitude in yourselves which was also in Christ Jesus, who, although He existed in the form of God, did not regard equality with God a thing to be grasped, but emptied Himself, taking the form of a bond-servant, and being made in the likeness of men. Being found in appearance as a man, He humbled Himself by becoming obedient to the point of death, even death on a cross.

—Philippians 2:5–8

The challenge of choosing to embrace humility in relationships with challenging people is that it will always involve a dying to self. Always. Jesus literally died on the cross; He was tortured and then was crucified in abject human pain. We were the difficult ones for whom He died. Humility bids us to die to ourselves. As you begin the journey toward humility, you will determine how bloody the death will be by how long you resist it … or choose to give in to it. You will need to die to opinions, preferences, comfort, and desires. You will die, my friend, make no mistake about it. Certain death always precedes the life of humility.

Humility is your *choice*. However, if you choose not to embrace this virtue as a lovely part of your emotional makeup, you will instead be choosing, by default, the traits of pride, bitterness, and arrogance.

Which way do you prefer to live?

In your quest to be a humble person who chooses to peacefully operate within the demands of a difficult relationship, remind yourself to respect the gifts and talents that God has placed within others. You will need to remember not to control every conversation, but instead become an interested listener. Rather than trying to jockey to be a person of importance, lay your ego on the altar of humility. Refuse to promote yourself with a heart attitude that honors God and then lavishly offer words of encouragement and blessing to the one who imposes upon you. The blessing will come back to you—I guarantee it!

Stronger Than You Think

The second character trait on Paul's list of worthy walking is the fruit of the Spirit known as gentleness. Don't be fooled by the softness that this word might portend; in actuality, gentleness is one of the strongest attributes that a person is able to embrace. Gentleness portrays the picture of a strong-willed person who has learned to submit his or her will to a higher authority. This disciplined control of gentle behavior has the capacity to be evident in many areas of life, including the words you choose to speak, the emotions you choose to exhibit, and the actions that you choose to take.

By nature, I am a gentle person ... but difficult people tend to abscond with my gentleness and deposit fierce frustration in its place. I must remind myself that it is in searing conversations with fractious people that I must choose the delicious fruit of gentleness. I must not allow someone else's harsh temperament to prevent me from being the joyful and gentle woman that Christ has called me to be.

The word *prautes*—which, you may recall, is the Greek word for an extremely patient gentleness—was used in ancient times in a medicinal sense. It described a soothing medication that had the healing potential to calm an angry wound or remove an infection. My friend, you and I are the soothing medication that the world needs to calm itself and remove the infection of bitterness and hatred. When we decide to be gentle rather than volatile, we are able to pour water on fiery emotions rather than the gasoline of our own tempers.

Never Explosive

The third character trait that Paul challenges us to embrace is patience. Oh my! This is where you might be tempted to close this book and never pick it up again, but don't do it! If you can develop the inner resolve to be patient with the most annoying person in your life, you will be living the life of your dreams.

Patience, which can also be defined as "long-suffering," is the Greek word *makrothumia*. Patience, like gentleness, is also a fruit of the Holy Spirit. *Makrothumia* paints the word picture of a candle with an extremely long wick that has the capacity to burn for a protracted time. This long-wicked candle will never explode, but it is a continual source of light and heat. This amazing candle is meant to be an image of you when you are struggling with a selfish person. This stunning candle is meant to be you when you are coping with a nasty person. This rare candle is meant to be you when you are striving with a loathsome person.

In Colossians, Paul reminded us to put patience on just like we would a favorite garment or an attractive piece of clothing. God has placed patience in your spiritual wardrobe and you get to choose it every day of your life! You will never regret wearing patience.

We urge you, brethren, admonish the unruly, encourage the faint-hearted, help the weak, be patient with everyone.

—1 Thessalonians 5:14

That about covers it, doesn't it?! We are reminded, once again, to be patient with everyone—and that certainly includes people who are like fingernails on the chalkboard of life. There is absolutely no one this side of heaven with whom it is *impossible* for you to be patient. You can be patient with your two-year-old, with your husband, with your mother-in-law, and with the person who works in the cubicle beside you. You can be patient with your boss, with your teenager, with your neighbor, and with your pastor. You can be patient because the God who has called you to patience will give you the strength to exhibit it. He's that kind of God!

Love is patient, love is kind and is not jealous; love does not brag and is not arrogant.   —1 Corinthians 13:4

In my own humanity, I am often impatient and frustrated with people who view life differently than I do. However, because of the unbeatable power of the Holy Spirit, I am more than able to be an unoffendable woman in every situation, in all conversations, and with all people.

I can be kind in situations that otherwise would bring out the worst in me.

I can be long-suffering in conversations that would otherwise frustrate me.

I can be Christlike because He lives within me.

Say It Again, Paul

When we studied the impact that Colossians 3 could have on our lives, do you recall that Paul instructed us to *"Bear with each other and forgive one another [and] … put on love"*? In the book of Ephesians, he says it in a different way, but with the same theme: *"Showing tolerance for one another in love."*

The word for "love" that Paul strategically uses in this verse is the Greek word *agape*, which means God's kind of love. God loved us when we were yet sinners.

But God demonstrates His own love toward us, in that while we were yet sinners, Christ died for us. —Romans 5:8

The word that is translated "tolerance" in this translation of Ephesians 4:2 is the Greek word *anecho*. At its core, this word means "to hold up, to sustain, to bear, and to endure." When we love a hard-to-please person, we are holding them up and helping them to endure. The miracle of it all is that love acts like a boomerang and it flies back to help us endure as well. Impatience will never help you sustain a relationship with a troublesome person, but love will always do so.

Paul and the Holy Spirit knew that we would encounter vicious relationships this side of heaven and so they offered to us God's opinion on the matter. You can take God's advice or not, but if I were you, I would enthusiastically embrace it! The Father certainly does know best.

Would you pray with me today:

Lord Jesus, I love You so much and I acknowledge my dependence upon You. Father, help me to be humble and not filled with pride. Help me to be gentle and not rough in my relationships with others. And most of all, Father, help me to exhibit patience and Your love every day of my life. In the incredible name of Jesus I pray. Amen.

To love another person is to see the face of God.
—Victor Hugo

23

Let It Begin with Me

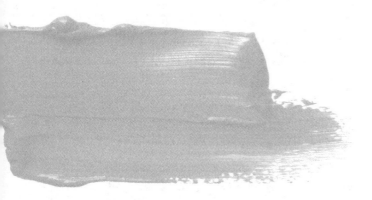

One of the grandest delights of my high school and college years was participating in choirs, both large and small.

I sang in the school ensembles from the time I was in third grade right through graduation day. I sang in the church choir before I was actually old enough to join and then never missed a church choir performance until I went away to college.

And then, joy of all joys, there were the days of singing in the university choir! To raise your voice in song with other men and women whose voices were trained and whose hearts were passionate about music was as close to heaven as I could get while I was still breathing.

A song that was sung by all of these choirs, from the youngest to the most proficient, was "Let There Be Peace on Earth."[9] As you read these lyrics, imagine being in the middle of a hundred-voice choir as they sing their hearts out to God and to anyone who would listen.

---

9. Jill Jackson and Sy Miller, "Let There Be Peace on Earth" (Jan-Lee Music, 1955).

Let there be peace on earth, and let it begin with me.
Let there be peace on earth, the peace that was meant to be.
With God as our Father, brothers all are we.
Let me walk with my brother in perfect harmony.

The line that touches me so deeply from this classic choral piece is the last one: *"Let there be peace on earth and let it begin with me!"*

Paul could have written these lyrics.

It Doesn't Just Happen

There are many things in life that are not accidents, nor are they certainties. Unity is one of those blessings in life that requires hard work and discipline. It doesn't *just happen* in a home, in a marriage, in an office, or in the church. Someone must make unity a high priority in order to achieve its status. Paul is begging us to be conscientious and earnest to preserve the virtue of peace.

Being diligent to preserve the unity of the Spirit in the bond of peace. —Ephesians 4:3

We all deeply desire peace in our relationships, especially in our families and in our marriages, but we must desire it desperately enough to make it a high priority. As a mother, when my children all lived at home, I was a ferocious warrior for peace in our family. I refused to allow fighting, bickering, back talk, or discord among the siblings. This quest was not an easy one but it was worth it. If one of my children was unkind to a brother or sister, the punishment was immediate with no explanation necessary. We only spoke words of kindness.

I would often ask one of the miniature McLeods, "Were those building words or destructive words?"

Unity in our home was important to me because I knew it was a high priority to the Father. The compelling truth is that unity in the home and peace in human relationships might be the most vital prerequisite to living abundantly this side of heaven. I refused to let my family be torn apart by selfish behavior or by lack of attention to the virtue of unity.

My husband Craig and I made date night a priority in our marriage so that there was unity in the leadership of our family. We were careful not to speak unkindly to one another in front of the children because we knew that our language modeled expected speech patterns to those who were listening to their parents.

We also were legalistic about setting aside a family night at least once a week. With five children of varying ages, it would have been easy to let the older ones make plans with their friends while the little ones stayed home in the care of a babysitter. But we insisted on a family night and attendance was not optional.

Now, in these young adult years, I observe my fully-grown children truly loving each other. They play games together and send hilarious text messages to each other. They no longer live at the same street address, but the compasses of their hearts all point to family.

It wasn't easy; there were many days that I wanted to throw up my hands and let each of them *do their own thing*. However, in the heart of a mother is the deep desire for unity and peace and I was not willing to settle for anything less than that.

UP: Unity and Peace

Unity and peace will always take your family, your marriage, your office, and your church in an upward direction. Unity and peace will always ensure that your life is continually traveling along the high roads of faith. Unity and peace create an invisible structure that will allow you to live, even with difficult people, in a manner that honors Christ.

Paul uses an interesting word as the verb in this *UP* phrase; he employs the word "preserve" to communicate fully what his expectations are. Paul requests that we be *"diligent to **preserve**"* unity in the sweet bonds of peace.

Whenever I happen upon the word "preserve" in my reading, I am always tempted to picture jars of my grandmother's delicious jams in her pantry, or my father's famous jars of pickles that lined the walls of our basement. However, in this verse, Paul is not referring to food or even to something perishable that requires preservation. Paul uses the Greek word *tereo*, which was a distinct military term in ancient Greece. It was a word that painted a picture of a military guard who was charged with the unarguable task of keeping watch over something or someone of extreme importance. These soldiers were not allowed to leave their post regardless of what attacks they encountered.

Paul has charged you to *tereo* unity in the bond of peace in all of your human relationships, but especially with those who share the same faith. Unity and peace are valuable and treasured resources in our families and in our friendships. Paul has not gently suggested that you preserve unity in the bond of peace, but he expects you to preserve it no matter who or what fights against you.

That's a mighty difficult assignment, isn't it? There have been numerous times in my life when I have greatly desired peace in a relationship, but the other person wasn't willing to work for it in the same diligent manner. What do you do when you are caught in the crossfire and human peace is simply not possible?

If possible, so far as it depends on you, be at peace with all men.
—Romans 12:18

In the moments when you have diligently guarded peace and even fought for peace but it just seems impossible, the most important goal is for you to have peace in your own heart. It is of vital importance that you are walking in forgiveness and blessing even when the other person continues to be argumentative or antagonistic. You can walk away knowing that you tried your hardest to *tereo* peace and still be kind to the other person involved in the challenging relationship.

If you truly long to live a vibrant life that is filled with joy and hope, then you must diligently fight for peace, but also realize that you need peace within your heart as well.

Often, when I have been engaged in a battle for peace, I remind myself that I am only allowed to say words that honor the Lord in a kind and non-judgmental manner. I have made a serious commitment to the Father that when relationships become sticky, I will forgive and bless the other person. I will not gossip nor will I enter into playing the blame game.

Peace is worth fighting for, it is worth forgiving for, and it is worth blessing the other person in spite of differences. What a wonderful way to approach difficult relationships! When peace is the goal and when the route is paved with forgiveness and blessing, the fulfillment will be unmatched. Peace is only truly experienced in human relationships when intimacy with Christ is valued and when we are surrendered to His ultimate and loving control.

The unalterable truth is that it is impossible to control everything that happens to you and it is futile to try to control the people in your life. The only thing that you can absolutely control is your response to painful situations and problematic people. Your power is found in your response; your peace is discovered when you respond the way that Jesus would.

Would you pray with me today:

Lord Jesus, I love You so much. Father, would You make me an instrument of Your peace? I pray that I will sow love where there is hatred and kindness where there is cruelty. Father, where confusion is found, would you allow me to be an ambassador of Your matchless peace? In Jesus's name I pray. Amen.

The more we sweat in peace, the less we bleed in war.
—Vijaya Lakshmi Pandit

24

Imitators

It is possible to be an imitator without being an imitation. Think about it for a minute! I can imitate a world-class chef to the most exact ingredient, measurement, and product ... but I am not an imitation of him. I can imitate a friend's laughter or another friend's spending habits, but that doesn't turn me into an imitation.

According to our good friend Noah Webster, an imitation is a counterfeit or a copy. While you are not called to be a counterfeit, you *are* called to imitate God, your Father, in every way that really matters in life. When you observe Him, through reading the Word of God, and then ask the Holy Spirit to make your life a mirror of His, you will be the grandest *you* imaginable!

When someone imitates God, it is as much about duplicating His actions as it is about disciplining their heart to matching His loving and kind heart. The call to live a vibrant life is not, at its core, about what you choose to do, but rather it is about who you choose to be. You are called to be like God.

His Heart Is My Heart

The next section of Scripture that we will study is also found in the stirring letter that Paul wrote to the church at Ephesus. His words echo through the ages and find a home in our hungry hearts today:

Therefore be imitators of God, as beloved children; and walk in love, just as Christ also loved you and gave Himself up for us, an offering and a sacrifice to God as a fragrant aroma.

—Ephesians 5:1–2

In this lovely piece of prose that was first birthed in the heart of the Holy Spirit, Paul presents yet another unarguable command: *"Therefore be imitators of God."*

It is impossible for a person to imitate someone whom they have never observed. In order for you to imitate the Father, you must observe Him— and the way that you are able to do that is by reading your Bible. If you want to know the heart of God, read the Word.

Because Your lovingkindness is better than life, my lips will praise You. —Psalm 63:3

The Bible—our source of all truth concerning the character and heart of the Father—declares that His lovingkindness is better than life! We need to imitate His lovingkindness that is more spectacular than the gift of life.

The LORD's lovingkindnesses indeed never cease, for His compassions never fail. They are new every morning; great is Your faithfulness. —Lamentations 3:22–23

We, as imitators of God, should never cease to be loving and kind; it is who He is and it should be who we are. We are called to be loving and kind to our children and to our spouses. We are challenged to be loving and kind to those of a different political persuasion. We are commanded to be loving and kind to difficult people and to cruel people.

I am so grateful that His mercy and compassions *"are new every morning."* Every day, when the clock turns to 12:01 a.m., the Lord has a new dose of mercy and compassion coming my way. He never runs out and neither should we. Every day when we awaken, we should pray, "Lord, give me a new download of who You are! Give me a gargantuan portion of mercy and compassion because I am going to need it today!"

The LORD *is gracious and merciful; slow to anger and great in lovingkindness.*   —Psalm 145:8

As the Lord's dearly loved children, we are the recipients of His kindness, grace, and mercy; as those who have been instructed to imitate Him, we should also be the vehicles through which His kindness, grace, and mercy flow. We should be splashing kindness on people like it's free—because it is! We should be running over with grace like it is abundant—because it is! We should be throwing around love like it is easy—because it is! And we should be slow to anger because we learned that from our Dad. The same Father who is slow to grow angry at your shortcomings will give you His emotional DNA to enable you to be slow to anger as well. The little petty annoyances of life should not have the power to rile your anger. When someone offends you, it should be met with mercy not with anger. When a person disagrees with you, your response should always be kindness rather than anger.

What a wonderful life we are called to drench ourselves in!

Naming Rights

My husband Craig and I agree on nearly everything in life—even when it comes to finances, food choices, and television shows. We have had no disagreements about raising our children, holiday celebrations, or whether or not to have pets. However, the one divisive issue in our heavenly marriage—approaching forty-five years!—was who should get to name the children.

I sweetly pointed out, in all of my pregnant glory, that Craig had established the last name for all of us, so shouldn't I, as the one going through nine months of fatigue, nausea, and sleeplessness, be the one with the honor of choosing the baby's name? I reminded him, with no guile in my voice, that I would also be the one going through the pain of labor while my body was torn apart from limb to limb in order to give birth to the nameless child.

Well, as you can probably guess by now, I didn't win the name battle … but we were able to compromise for all five of our children's names. The *Great McLeod Compromise* was determined by the meaning of the name that we chose for each child. When it came down to it, meaning was more important to both of us, as parents, than was the actual name itself.

Our firstborn son was named Matthew Craig because *Matthew* means *gift of God* and we deeply desired to honor the Lord with our firstborn's name. Then, when little boy number two came along, we named him Christopher Burton. *Christopher* means *bearer of Christ* and Burton was chosen to honor my father as it was my maiden name.

Then came little boy number three. The truth is, I had allowed Craig to have the final say in choosing our other sons' names, so this time, it was my turn—right?! Craig, being the darling, Southern gentleman that he is, finally acquiesced to my choice of *Jordan*, which means *the one who carries on*. We fully believed that Jordan would carry on for us in the family ministry.

And then, joy of all joys! We finally had a baby girl. Her name is Carolyn Joy, but we have called her *Joy-Belle* since the instant she was born. I always tell young moms that *Joy* is what you name a little girl after three rambunctious boys.

And then came our surprise! Baby number five was another precious little girl, and quite frankly, I was out of names by then. We named her Joni

Rebecca after both of her grandmothers and she has been a fitting beneficiary of their strength of character and faith.

You must remind yourself often that only the One who has created you
has the power to give you a name. What child do you know who has named
himself or herself? That thought, of having the right to name yourself, is
utterly absurd, isn't it? Your past doesn't have the right to give you a name,
your sin has no naming rights, and certainly your environment can't name
you. Only the One who has created you has the authority to give you the
name of His choosing—and God's name for you is *Beloved*.

You are so unconditionally and thoroughly loved by the One who
fathered you that He could think of no better or more appropriate name
than the precious identity of Beloved, which in Greek is *agapetos*. The root
of this word is *agape*, which describes the love of God toward His children.
Agape is an unconditional, thorough, complete, and enthusiastic love from
the Father that blankets us with His character. *Agapetos*, which is your
God-given name, means "beloved, esteemed, dear, favorite, worthy of love."

I hope that starting today, you will wear your name, Beloved, with
honor and joy. I hope that you will declare your name out loud when the
enemy tries to rename you with a lie. My prayer is that you will know who
you are and you will know the God whom you are imitating.

Would you pray with me today:

Lord Jesus, thank You for naming me *Beloved*. I accept Your
love and Your favor today. I pray that You will use me as a
vessel to share Your love with others. And Dad, I want to be
just like You! In Jesus's name I pray. Amen.

~

He who is filled with love is filled with God Himself.
—Augustine of Hippo

25

Learning to Walk Again

Afew years ago, I suffered from a very serious hip issue. I am a disciplined daily walker and the pain was intense. I could barely get out of bed in the morning; I would hobble downstairs in excruciating pain and then sit in a recliner all day long. I hated every minute of it! My husband took me to a physical therapist, a chiropractor, and an orthopedist, but nothing seemed to help me at all. I was loaded up with pain pills, exercises, and a chart that showed me what position to sleep in.

After nearly a year of the pain and inability to exercise, I went to yet another doctor, who told me, "Yes, you do have a tear in your hip labrum, but it will heal eventually. You just have developed some bad walking habits and you need to learn how to walk again."

This doctor showed me how to walk correctly. She told me to take smaller steps, slow down, and focus on my foot placements. My pain didn't disappear overnight, but over the course of a month or two, it was gone and it has never come back. So in my sixties, I learned how to walk again!

The Love Walk

Therefore be imitators of God, as beloved children; and walk in love, just as Christ also loved you and gave Himself up for us, an offering and a sacrifice to God as a fragrant aroma.

—Ephesians 5:1–2

We now know that we are called to imitate our Father and we also know our true identity as *Beloved*. There is yet another riveting challenge in this verse that we are called to participate in this side of heaven. We are invited by the Holy Spirit to participate in the *love walk*. This is a walk that might challenge you at first and you might have to dispense with some bad habits, but once you get the hang of it, you will realize that this is the very best way to walk through life!

Once learned, the *love walk* will become an effective and delightful habit! Rather than responding to people emotionally, you will embrace the joy of responding to them with love, which, as you know, is a delicious fruit of the Holy Spirit.

When your spouse gets on your nerves, you smile and say, "Sure do love you today, honey!" That's the love walk!

When the server at the drive-through window gets your order wrong again, you respond with, "I sure appreciate your service to me and so many others. Have a great day!" That's the love walk!

When someone pulls out in front of you in traffic, rather than laying on the horn and saying words under your breath so that the children can't hear you, pray out loud and bless the person. That's the love walk!

When your two-year-old displays behavior that is totally in line with being a two-year-old, rather than screaming at your darling child, you take his little face in your hands and say, "Mommy sure does love you! You are going to grow up to be a phenomenal young man!" That's the love walk!

When in doubt, my friend, simply choose to walk in love. Don't be led by your feelings, your opinions, or by past mistreatment, but love everyone more than they deserve to be loved. God, after all, loves you *eternally* more than you deserve to be loved and the Scripture has instructed us to imitate Him. That's the love walk!

Your world will shift beneath your feet when you realize how enthusiastically the Father loves you and therefore how much love you have to give to others. You can't hoard His generous gift of love; you must share it with the world in which you live. It is why you are here to live for yet another day. *Jesus needs you to love like He loves.*

The Smell of Death

Jesus had to die in order to demonstrate His extreme and unending love for me. Therefore, I, too, might need to die to the flesh at times in order to demonstrate my love for others. I might need to die to preferences or opinions; I might need to die to my emotions or creature comforts.

All dying creatures have a certain odor about them, don't they? You, too, will have an odor that identifies your glorious sacrifice of love to the world around you. However, your odor will not be vile or putrid, but a sweet-scented bouquet for your Father. Your life will become an aromatic perfume of love that brings joy and delight to the Father's heart.

Imitating the Father is a delectable portion of what enables you to live a vibrant and joyful life. Knowing that you were named Beloved and accepting His identification of you will deliver energy and a sparkle to your life that is magnetic. When you *"walk in love,"* you will have a spring in your step and a confidence that is adorable. And when you die to self in order to love others, you will fill the Father's throne room with the fragrance of heavenly flowers!

Would you pray with me today:

Lord Jesus, I need You! I need Your strength and Your power to love the people in my life. Lord, I refuse to settle for anything less than Your unconditional love flowing through me toward others. In Jesus's name I pray. Amen.

The love of God and the God of love constrain you to love one another that it may at last be said of Christians as it was at first, "Behold! How they love one another!"
—Ralph Venning

PART SIX

It's Enough

26

Do It Again, Self

Are you ready to giggle or chuckle with me for just a minute? I honestly do not know how to introduce this next portion of Scripture without saying, "It's my favorite!" The verses that we are about to mine for pure gold are among the most beloved verses in the entire New Testament. I am asking the Holy Spirit to make them alive and fresh in you today! I pray that He will give us a double portion of revelation knowledge as we gaze in wonder at the magnificence of these six ancient yet timeless verses.

Rejoice in the Lord always; again I will say, rejoice! Let your gentle spirit be known to all men. The Lord is near. Be anxious for nothing, but in everything by prayer and supplication with thanksgiving let your requests be made known to God. And the peace of God, which surpasses all comprehension, will guard your hearts and your minds in Christ Jesus. Finally, brethren, whatever is true, whatever is honorable, whatever is right, whatever is pure, whatever is lovely, whatever is of good repute, if there is any excellence and if anything worthy of praise, dwell on these things. The things you have learned and received and heard and seen in me, practice these things, and the God of peace will be with you.

—Philippians 4:4–9

If there were only six verses in the Epistles of the New Testament, the above verses would be enough. Packed inside this sextuplet of phrases is enough power, instruction, and challenge for you to completely live the life of your dreams. Let's get started!

Rewind

Paul is a broken record when it comes to encouraging believers in all generations to *"rejoice in the Lord"*! These four little words hold the entire theme of Paul's letter to the church at Philippi.

I have often thought that if anyone had the right to complain, it was Paul. Once again, he's in prison, writing a letter to a group of believers. If anyone had a right to talk about how depressed he was or how unfair life was, it was certainly Paul! If anyone had the right to complain about life, about unfair treatment, or about not walking in his destiny, it was unarguably Paul. If anyone had the right to blame God, it was Paul.

But instead of blaming or complaining, Paul says, "Rejoice!" What a man this former persecutor of Christians has become! Paul not only issues the injunction to rejoice, but is so emphatic that he repeats himself: *"Again I will say, rejoice!"*

Paul is teaching a monumental lesson in this one verse; he is teaching all of Christendom, including you and me, that our inner attitudes do not have to reflect our outward circumstances. Emotionally healthy and vibrant people know that this one determinant is a solid secret to living a vibrant life.

When you have the moxie to embrace a lifestyle of sheer joy despite rotten circumstances, you are declaring to all of the demons in hell and to all the angels in heaven, "I *know* that my God will bring good out of absolutely everything that comes my way!"

When you have the audacity to rejoice rather than rant, you are drawing a line in that infamous sand that declares, "My God is more than able to protect me in a prison, to deliver me out of a storm, and to promote me in every challenge in life."

Paul's voice echoes through the ages as he coaches you and me to, *"Rejoice in the Lord always!"* Paul knew what we often ignore: there is *always* something to be grateful for. If you are missing joy in your life, then make a list of blessings for which you are grateful. Joy and thanksgiving are not so very far apart. When you choose to be a thankful person, I can guarantee you that joy is on its way to the front door of your heart.

Paul and I are not encouraging you to *pretend* to be happy, but we are stating the fact of faith that all pilgrims who came before us discovered: we are a people who find our joy in the Lord, not in our circumstances. Your ability to live an overcoming life is discovered in your ability to choose joy regardless of your circumstances.

I have made joy a discipline of my life, just like brushing my teeth and drinking a cup of coffee in the morning. I have discovered that reading the Word and then declaring the Word out loud chases away depression and opens the door to joy. I have ascertained that listening to worship music and commanding myself to rejoice in the Lord might not change my circumstances, but it *always* changes me.

Paul not only orders believers to rejoice in the Lord, but he also tells them exactly *when* to do it. He is specific and practical in this command, *"Rejoice in the Lord always!"*

The word *always* in this sentence is a part of speech that grammarians identify as *an absolute*, defined as "expressing finality with no implication of possible change."

Paul's command to rejoice in the Lord always will never change no matter how much you disagree with him. You can whine, complain, contradict, or mutter under your breath, but Paul's advice is absolutely final.

Christians are commanded to rejoice always! And if you didn't understand it the first time, Paul repeated it just for your learning pleasure: *"Again I will say, rejoice!"*

He Is Near

Have you noticed how children act differently when their parents are around? Have you noticed how students respond differently to a strict teacher rather than to a lenient one? If you knew that the Lord was near, how would that change your behavior?

Let your gentle spirit be known to all men. The Lord is near.
—Philippians 4:5

If we, as children of our loving Father, truly believe that the Lord is near to us, we would probably treat others differently, wouldn't we? If we actually believed that Jesus was listening in on every conversation, wouldn't we change the words we use and the tone of voice in which we say those words? I have learned that it is not my opinion that matters the most, but rather how I actually treat other people. The encouragement that Paul now gives to be a gentle person is powerful and tender at the same time.

In Paul's conversation with the church at Philippi, he is simply stating the importance of being gracious in our treatment of others and reminding us to compassionately understand their weaknesses.

Unfortunately, we have bought into the cultural falsehood that in order for a person to change, it is up to you and me to demand that they change. We inaccurately think that we have the right to ventilate our opinions concerning another person's weakness all over their personhood. I have often called this type of behavior *verbal vomit*. We fictitiously conclude that listing all of the ways that we are right and that they are wrong is going to change the situation.

May I just submit to you today that God really *does* know best? Perhaps it is your gentleness that will enable a person to change.

If you don't know how to respond to a difficult person, you might try being gentle. If you don't know how to treat an opinionated person, perhaps you should take God's advice and be gentle. When someone gets on your very last nerve, my advice to you is to be gentle. When you are the victim of someone's mistreatment, pray about being gentle in return.

You and I are unaware of the battle that others are fighting. Everyone has been mistreated in ways that we know absolutely nothing about. Everyone with whom we come into contact has hidden wounds ... and our gentleness is the healing salve for their desperate aches.

The Lord is near, my friend. He is closer than you could ever imagine. He is listening in on every conversation and watching every action. He sees you roll your eyes at your husband and weeps as you scream at your two-year-old. Can you hear Paul reminding you to be gentle?

Today is a new day, a gentle day. He is near.

Would you pray with me today:

Lord Jesus, I repent. Forgive me for being rough and judgmental with people. Thank You that today is a new day and I get to start all over again. With Your divine help, I recommit to having a gentle tongue, a gentle countenance, and a gentle voice. In Jesus's precious name I pray. Amen.

⌒

I choose gentleness ... nothing is won by force. I choose to be
gentle. If I raise my voice may it be only in praise.
If I clench my fist, may it be only in prayer. If I make a
demand, may it be only of myself.
—Max Lucado

27

What a Relief

As I look back at the years of my life, it is easy for me to recognize the fact that nothing has had a more profound effect on me than the Word of God. I was raised in a stable, loving, Christian home and I know that not everyone is blessed with that type of upbringing. However, being raised at the knee of a general of the faith is not the most significant aspect of my life. I have been married to a godly, kind man for more than forty years and I am fully aware that not every person has had the type of marriage with which I have been gifted. However, my Christian marriage is not even the most impressive blessing that I have been given.

The most impactful gift of my entire life has been the Bible—and wonder of all wonders, we all have access to it! The blessing of reading the Bible is not mine alone, but it is offered to everyone. Our lives can all be stabilized and encouraged by the Word of God. Nothing will solidify your life like the Bible will. Absolutely nothing else has the strengthening power of the Word of God. There is no person, no degree, or no opportunity that will set you upon the road of your destiny quite like the Bible has the capacity to do. And we all have it! We all have the Bible!

The following words that Paul gently speaks to us over the hallways of time often make me cry as I use them to evaluate my own life. There are also days when I read these familiar words and smile, knowing that Paul *gets me*. I will also admit that when my heart settles down and drinks in these verses, I am often forced to stand on my spiritual tiptoes because of the challenge that Paul offers. Whether these words cause you to smile, to cry, or to sweat, I hope that most of all, they cause you to pray.

> *Be anxious for nothing, but in everything by prayer and supplication with thanksgiving let your requests be made known to God. And the peace of God, which surpasses all comprehension, will guard your hearts and your minds in Christ Jesus.*
> —Philippians 4:6–7

Nothing

If we are honest, we all have intense moments in life when anxiety creeps in like an uninvited guest and endeavors to abscond with our peace, our joy, and our hope. In prayer gatherings, I have often heard people pray fretfully rather than filled with faith. Allow me to assure you today that God does not respond to your worries, but He responds in power to your faith.

Paul uses the Greek word *merimnao* in this verse, which means "to be troubled; to be anxious; to be fretful; to be worried about something." *Merimnao* is the same word that Matthew used in writing about Jesus's well-known Sermon on the Mount, when He taught:

> *For this reason I say to you, do not be **worried** about your life, as to what you will eat or what you will drink; nor for your body, as to what you will put on. Is not life more than food and the body more than clothing? Look at the birds of the air, that they do not*

sow, nor reap nor gather into barns, and yet your heavenly Father feeds them. Are you not worth much more than they?

—Matthew 6:25–26

"*Do not be worried.*" The very words of Jesus, the Son of the living God, ricochet through ages and land in our hearts. He tells us, "Stop worrying about the small stuff in life! Don't be anxious about the things that you see and don't fret about your circumstances! I have it all under control!"

Merimnao appears again in the parable of the sower:

---

*And the one on whom seed was sown among the thorns, this is the man who hears the word, and the **worry** of the world and the deceitfulness of wealth choke the word, and it becomes unfruitful.*

—Matthew 13:22

This is a sobering verse for me, as a woman who loves the Word of God but also wrestles with worry from time to time. I can hear the gentle voice of Jesus looking at the pockets of anxiety in my human heart and warning me, "Carol, I know that you love the Bible, but let Me just tell you that when you worry, it will strangle the fruitfulness of God in your life." That's a sobering thought, isn't it, my friend?

Paul's words to the Philippians are not a mere suggestion; he is seriously pleading with all of us who identify as Christians not to be worried about our circumstances or about the things that we see with our natural eyes. Paul is reminding us with fervor not to allow the events of our lives to throw us into an anxiety attack or cause a nervous meltdown. While our Bible translates his words as, "*Be anxious for nothing,*" Paul actually qualifies this statement with the Greek word *meden*, which means "absolutely nothing."

Meden is an absolute in the Greek language; Paul is declaring to the church then and now, "There is not one event, person, or circumstance that should draw you into a season of worry or anxiety. Nothing! Not anytime! Not any place! Not anywhere! Nothing! Zero! Zilch! Nada!"

If you struggle with anxiety, perhaps you could incorporate just a few habits into your life that might help you when the uneasy thoughts begin to invade your mind.

+ Talk to a friend who will listen to your heart and who will also pray with you.

+ Quote a favorite Bible verse out loud.

+ Listen to worship music and sing along.

+ Put your phone away for at least an hour while you read a devotional or your Bible, and then spend time in prayer.

+ Go outside for a walk in the fresh air.

+ Serve someone else. Do something kind for someone in your life.

+ Spend some time just counting your blessings.

You might need to eventually go for counseling, which is nothing to be ashamed of at all! If counseling helps you deal with anxiety, then please consider it today.

I have heard it said that we, as Christians, are identified as believers and not as worriers. As Christians, believing in God is what we do best! We believe in a God who is able to work all things together for our highest good and for His glory. Do you believe it? Then quit worrying!

We are invited to rejoice, but we are cautioned not to worry!

Everything

The third absolute in this portion of Scripture is the word *everything* and it serves as a call to worship and prayer that will undergird your life with strength.

In everything by prayer and supplication with thanksgiving let your requests be made known to God. —Philippians 4:6

Paul issues an amazing proposition that is difficult to turn down if you desire for your life to be meaningful and rich. And, once again, he tells us exactly when we are supposed to respond to this delightful discipline. How I love the heart of Paul and the change that his words and his advice have made in my life!

We are ushered into the very presence of God while we are still sucking in the oxygen of earth if we pray, petition God humbly, and give thanks in *everything*. The word *everything* that Paul uses means:

+ All the time

+ Everywhere

+ In every situation

+ For all things

+ Every time

+ In every place

+ All that exists

+ All that is important

Everything is an absolute, which means it encompasses all, with nothing left out!

Paul insists that we are a people who should pray all the time rather than worry anytime. Prayer is when an ordinary person spends time in the presence of the Creator of the earth. When I am with Him, my worries don't seem so worrisome. It is impossible for me to worry in His presence because I am captured by His magnificence!

Prayer is an intimate word and it implies a sweet closeness with the Father. Please don't spend another long night lying awake and worrying, but spend it in relishing all of the facets of His character. Enjoy the Father and stay close to Him all the time.

Paul also summons believers to supplicate at all times. Supplication is a type of prayer that is insistent and passionate, heartfelt and earnest. It is when we cry out, "Help!" to the Father at a dire moment in life. One of the stirring lessons that I have learned in the classroom of prayer is that I don't have to be good at it; I just have to *mean it* to get the job done.

When you face a problem, you are never allowed to worry about it, but you are always encouraged to come face to face with God the Father and cry out for His help. When the world around you is crashing in and you are in desperate need of divine intervention, you are summoned by the Holy Spirit to become very bold and cry out for God to move on your behalf. Worry never works, but supplication always works.

When I find the need to go to the Father in an intense manner, I always arm myself with the Word of God and I tell the Lord what Scriptures I am standing on in that situation. I remind the Father of His promises to me. I push my way into the throne room with His written constitution in my hand and in my mouth.

The third type of prayer that we are pressed into by Paul is thanksgiving. All of the time is an appropriate time to praise the Lord! Praise never goes out of style; you can never give God too much of it and it's always meaningful. One of my grandest goals in the prayer room of my heart is to be just as passionate in my thanksgiving as I am in my supplication. I long to praise Him more than I want anything in my catalogue of human desires.

All

When we accept the invitation of the Holy Spirit to refuse anxiety and to perpetually pray, supplicate, and give thanks, there is a benefit that begins to head straight toward us as a result.

And the peace of God, which surpasses all comprehension, will guard your hearts and your minds in Christ Jesus.
—Philippians 4:7

You won't understand the peace of God, but you will receive it when you refuse to worry and when you spend your life praying, supplicating, and giving thanks. The peace of God will override every human thought that you have and will act as a buffer for all of life's problems. The peace that we receive from the Father is not based on our circumstances, but it is based on His character. He is the Prince of Peace. In the Old Testament, God the Father is identified as Jehovah-Shalom or the Lord our Peace.

The peace that is ours through Christ does not come delivered through perfect or serene circumstances, but it is a peace that rules in our hearts when we quietly acknowledge that He works all things together for our good and for His glory. (See Romans 8:28.) It is a peace that is never delivered without His presence.

Your mind is command central for every other area of your life. Your mind controls your bodily functions, your bodily systems, and your speech patterns. Your mind tells your heart to beat, your eyes to blink, and your tongue to talk. God's peace is more powerful than your brain could ever be! God's peace is so superior to your mind that it tells your mind to sit down and be quiet!

When you stop that nasty habit of fretting and then begin the delightful discipline of rejoicing, praying, supplicating, and giving thanks, you receive the most valuable treasure of your entire life—the peace of God!

The Greek word that is translated as *"guard"* in Philippians 4:7 was a military phrase that described the faithful soldiers overseeing every person who was allowed to go into or out of a city. God's peace acts much like that fine contingent of devoted soldiers. His peace will ensure that nothing goes into your brain or is allowed to linger there unless His peace allows it. The enemy has lost his access to your valuable thought life when you choose to rejoice, pray, supplicate, and give thanks.

Would you pray with me today:

Lord Jesus, thank You for Your peace that surpasses all understanding. I refuse to worry and I joyfully welcome Your amazing peace into my thought life. I give You permission, Father, to allow Your peace to rule and reign inside of me. I need Your peace and so I accept it today in the name of Jehovah-Shalom. Amen.

Peace reigns where our Lord reigns.
—Julian of Norwich

28

Something to Think About

I am so grateful that people aren't able to read my mind, aren't you? What a woeful discovery that would be if everywhere that I went, someone had the superpower to look into my brain with a type of X-ray vision and have the capacity to discern every single one of my thoughts. How embarrassing! How humiliating! How awkward!

My thought life is very spectacular at times, but at other moments, it looks and smells much like the town dump. I can embrace the finest of thoughts for a while … and then suddenly my brain is invaded with hopelessness, doubt, negativity, and foolishness. My brain needs help—and Paul is just the man to give it!

Concentration

The Holy Spirit and Paul have literally ganged up on us in this next verse. The Holy Spirit has given Paul permission to write a list of the only topics that we should think about while on this journey called life.

Finally, brethren, whatever is true, whatever is honorable, whatever is right, whatever is pure, whatever is lovely, whatever is of good repute, if there is any excellence and if anything worthy of praise, dwell on these things. —Philippians 4:8

Two verses earlier, Paul cautioned us not to allow thoughts of worry, fret, or anxiety to enter the vast expanse of our mind. In this verse, he does an about-face and rather than telling us what we should *not* think about, Paul tells us of the amazing thoughts that *should* be filling our brains! This amazing checklist will keep you out of the swamp of troublesome thinking for the rest of your life.

You might believe that your thought life has no determining power concerning how you actually live your life, but that is decisively false.

For as [a man] *thinks within himself, so he is.* —Proverbs 23:7

The thoughts that you choose to think today become the reality of your life tomorrow. If you think angry, critical thoughts today, I can assure you that your life tomorrow will not be joyful or hopeful. If your mind is filled with worry and anxiety today, then you have no hope for living a peaceful and gentle life tomorrow. Your thought life has more power in determining your probability of living a vibrant life than you can imagine!

Paul has offered a checklist of the appropriate thoughts that you should be thinking all day long every day of your life. You don't get to worry but you are cordially invited to have a mind that is filled with:

+ True thoughts

+ Honorable thoughts

+ Righteous thoughts

+ Pure thoughts

+ Lovely thoughts

+ Good reports or commendable thoughts

+ Excellent thoughts

+ Praiseworthy thoughts

Paul and the Holy Spirit have given us an amazing list of ideas for our thought lives. If we focus on placing only these types of thoughts in our minds, we won't have time to worry, be critical, or fantasize anymore. Perhaps rather than focusing on what we are not allowed to think about, our focus should be on all of the magnificent things that we *do* get to think about!

You need to put your thought life through a simple quiz on a daily basis. You should examine any and every thought that comes into your brain by asking it these simple questions:

+ Is it a true thought?

+ Does this thought express honor?

+ Is this a righteous thought?

+ Is this a pure thought or a nasty thought?

+ Is this thought lovely? Does it add to the beauty of my thought life or subtract from it?

+ Does this thought hold a good report? Is it commendable?

+ Does this thought make my brain excellent or mediocre?

+ Does this thought bring praise to the Lord?

If a thought can pass this test, then you get to think about it! One of the most beautiful parts of evaluating one's thought life is that when your thoughts are submitted to God's ideas, you will become what you are thinking about! You will become a truthful, honorable, righteous, pure, lovely, commendable, excellent, and praiseworthy person! It is all part of the journey that you are on to live a vibrant life filled with the wealth of the character and promises of the Father.

Would you pray with me today:

Lord Jesus, I want to have Your mind! I long to think Your thoughts! Today, Father, I declare that I will think only thoughts of truth, honor, righteousness, purity, loveliness, good report, excellence, and praise! In Jesus's lovely name I pray. Amen.

Watch your thoughts, they become words; watch your words, they become actions; watch your actions, they become habits; watch your habits, they become character; watch your character, for it becomes your destiny.
—Frank Outlaw

29

He Is with You

One of the most intimate and sweetest aspects of the invitation to live a vibrant life is simply the realization that *God is with you.* How can anything be too difficult when you realize that the One who knows you the best and loves you the most has promised to always be at your side?

It's Your Turn

Paul's concluding statement in the passage that has challenged us in our thinking, our worshipping, and our praying is this:

The things you have learned and received and heard and seen in me, practice these things, and the God of peace will be with you.
—Philippians 4:9

As I picture Paul writing these words from a Roman prison cell, I can imagine that he realizes that he needs to pass his mantle to those who will come after him. Paul was acutely aware that believers all over the ancient world had been closely observing his life as he preached, wrote, spent time in prison, dealt with storms and shipwrecks, was persecuted for the cause of Christ, and encouraged those under his watch. Now it was time for a new generation of believers to lead with honor and a Christlike demeanor.

Paul's stirring advice to those who would come after him is the same advice that he would give to us today in the twenty-first century.

+ Rejoice!

+ Be gentle

+ Be anxious for nothing

+ Pray

+ Supplicate

+ Think truthful and noble thoughts

You Can't Shake Him!

Finally, Paul reminded those to whom he was writing, *"The God of peace will be with you."* And in those words, we discover the blessed assurance that encouraged Paul's heart and mind no matter his circumstances. I pray that those words that Paul wrote as a blessing over the early church will resonate in your heart as well.

You are never alone, my friend! The Lord's presence is guiding you, watching you, and protecting you. You have been given the treasured gift of not only His peace, but also Him!

I will never desert you, nor will I ever forsake you.

—Hebrews 13:5

Elisabeth Elliot, one of my heroines of the faith, wrote a sentence in one of her many books that has impacted me greatly over the years:

When you feel abandoned and alone, you must preach to yourself the gospel of the boundless, eternal and unshakable love of God.

You couldn't shake the presence of God even if you tried to do so for the rest of your life! God, your heavenly Father, is the first helicopter parent in all of recorded history!

One of the most cherished aspects of life this side of heaven is friendship with Jesus. Time with Jesus turns an awful day into an amazing day.

When I settle down and spend time in prayer alone with Jesus, it revolutionizes a mediocre day into a magnificent day.

When I choose to read the Word and ignore the distractions in my world, it delivers the peace that passes understanding.

When I choose to sing myself to sleep rather than cry myself to sleep, it ushers me into His presence, where there is always fullness of joy.

Do not ignore the gift you have been given in Him! Paul's God is your God and He is with you today just like He was with Paul in prison.

Would you pray with me today:

Jesus, I love You so much. Thank You for Your continual presence in my life. You are my favorite Person to be with! Jesus, would You use me, just like You used Paul, to leave an impact on the next generation? I am Yours, Lord. In the name of Jesus, my Best Friend, I pray. Amen.

I don't always feel His presence. But God's promises do not depend upon my feelings; they rest upon His integrity.
—R. C. Sproul

PART SEVEN

Being Not Doing

30

The Miracle of Multiplication

Sometimes I grow tired of myself. I become weary in messing up, in saying the wrong things, in showing my impatience, and in being too hard on the people I love. Sometimes, I simply get exasperated with me, myself, and I! Now, don't worry about me; it's not that I am throwing chairs at people or using profanity. Often, my turmoil is an inner one that no one can see but me. However, I am fully aware that my heart is stumbling and it should not be so.

We are now going to spend some time with Peter and learn from his unique perspective on life. If we choose to wrap ourselves in the habits and attitudes that Peter promotes, the Holy Spirit promises that we will never stumble again! We all need to experience the life change that Peter experienced nearly 2,000 years ago.

A Man Named Peter

Peter and his brother Andrew had heard the voice of Jesus call them away from their stinky fishing boats to follow Him. They left behind their source of income, most likely their families, and all that was familiar in order to follow the Lord.

Most theologians describe Peter as fiery, impetuous, and opinionated. Peter was known for speaking before he thought. He was the disciple who cut off a soldier's ear, had the nerve to rebuke the Lord, and then denied Christ three times just before He was crucified. Peter was also the only disciple with enough bravado to walk on the water with Christ.

I have always had a special place in my heart for Peter—and it might be because I am so much like him. I have often dealt with loud opinions, roller-coaster emotions, and lack of control with my tongue. However, after Jesus rose from the dead, Peter was no longer filled with self but filled with godly wisdom. What changed this combustible man?

I believe that two things transformed Peter from being bullheaded to becoming composed. First of all, Peter saw the risen Lord with his very own eyes! And secondly, Peter had been filled with the Holy Spirit at Pentecost. I believe those two things—encountering the Lord and being filled with the Holy Spirit—are guaranteed to change any one of us!

When Peter wrote his epistles, he was the leader of the New Testament church. He truly had become, as Jesus had prophesied, the rock upon which Christ could build his church.

Peter had been changed from an ordinary fisherman with fish guts under his fingernails to a world-renowned evangelist. Peter was transformed from impetuous to rock solid. He was revolutionized from a denier to a proclaimer. The same Holy Spirit that changed Peter from the inside out is able to do this for each one of us as well!

This apostle wrote the epistle of 2 Peter in order to encourage the believers who would be facing fierce trials from the Roman government, from the Jewish leaders, and from their very own families. This book of the New Testament was written in about 64 AD from Rome when the great persecution under Nero was just beginning. Christians were literally being hunted down and killed for their faith in Christ. The church in Jerusalem was being scattered across the ancient world.

If a believer took the dangerous risk of being baptized at this moment in history, other believers in the Lord formed a celebratory parade through the streets of their village. They held torches high in the air and waved palm branches as they sang the brand new songs of their faith. As a follower of Christ waded into the waters to make his or her faith public, he or she would shout, "I renounce the devil and all of his ways!"

Often, the Roman soldiers were waiting for the newly baptized believer as they waded out of the waters. The new converts were sometimes killed; often, they were thrown into prison and had to watch as their children were killed. This is the church to which Peter wrote his passionate and clear letter.

Peter was actually crucified only about three years after writing this practical and powerful book. He asked to be crucified upside down because he believed he was not worthy to be crucified in the same manner as his Master.

This book was written to people who understand that heaven is only a breath away and yet are determined to live at full throttle for Christ and His kingdom while on planet earth. Peter calls all of us to live simply vibrantly!

Know God

The words of Peter, written nearly 2,000 years ago, are living and active today; they aim straight for the foundational issues of our lives:

Grace and peace be multiplied to you in the knowledge of God and of Jesus our Lord; seeing that His divine power has granted to us everything pertaining to life and godliness, through the true knowledge of Him who called us by His own glory and excellence.

—2 Peter 1:2–3

What a wonderful and breathtaking thought our friend Peter gives us! He introduces his encouragement to bullied believers from every generation by reminding us that our grace and peace will be multiplied as we get to know Jesus the Son and God the Father better. I need more grace and peace every day of my life and rather than claw for it or die from lack of it, what I really need to do is focus on my friendship with the Creator and my Savior.

As I study the Word and spend time meditating on Scriptures, I will find that the grace and the peace within me are being stirred up. As I develop a rich and intimate prayer life and develop the ability to hear the voice of God, I will discover that I am no longer starving for grace or being ravaged by lack of peace. Friendship with the Father and brotherhood with the Son has a direct bearing on the grace that I exhibit to others and the peace that is guarding my mind.

I must know Him! I must cultivate an ever-deepening and perpetually exciting relationship with Jesus. What a joy this invitation holds! If I believe nothing else, I believe that friendship with Jesus is the absolute foundation in my quest to live a life of vibrancy and power. Every other positive and godly characteristic in my life will cease to grow if I don't make Him my priority.

You've Got It!

One of the most exciting and stirring aspects of my faith is the realization that Jesus didn't leave us down here in the crossfire of good versus evil to fend for ourselves. He didn't die for us and then desert us. He refused to go to heaven without leaving us with everything that we would need to live triumphantly, victoriously, and vibrantly! Everything! *"Seeing that His divine power has granted to us **everything** pertaining to life and godliness...."*

I know that every word in the Holy Bible is God-inspired and God-breathed, *"sharper than any two-edged sword"* (Hebrews 4:12). However, I must tell you that there are some particular phrases in the Word of God that absolutely send my soul into a state of unmatched delight and excitement. Peter's words regarding everything that God has given us is one of those verses that just penetrates the heart of my issues every single time that I read it.

Peter states that the *power of God* has already been given to us; it is not a future hope but a current reality. The power of creation, the power that parted the Red Sea, and the power that kept the three Hebrew boys safe in a raging fire is the power that has already been given to us. The power that multiplied five loaves and two tiny fish to feed a ravenous crowd, the power that healed the woman who had bled for twelve long years, the power that raised Lazarus from the dead—*that* power is the heartbeat of our daily certainty. The power that raised Christ from the dead and the power that was given on the day of Pentecost has been generously donated by the Father to revolutionize our daily walk!

The very reason that Paul declared, *"I can do all things through Him who strengthens me"* (Philippians 4:13) is because he knew the same power that Peter is now declaring to the persecuted church.

Paul also stated that in Christ, *"all the fullness of Deity dwells in bodily form, and in Him you have been made complete, and He is the head over all rule and authority"* (Colossians 2:9–10).

When you have Jesus and the power that He converts into your life, you will never lack for anything again. You have been generously given every single thing that you need to live a vibrant life this side of heaven's shores.

The power that Peter is teaching is the same power that Paul declared. It is a power that is at once both practical and invincible.

When Paul wrote of this same power to his young disciple Timothy, he reminded him, *"The Spirit God gave us does not make us timid, but gives us power, love and self-discipline"* (2 Timothy 1:7 NIV).

According to both Peter and Paul—the two most impressive voices in the early church—the power that God has generously given to us should make a difference in the way we live on a daily basis in a practical way.

The power that is now yours should make a difference in the way you parent, in the way you treat your husband or wife, in your work ethic, and in your devotional life. The power of Christ should never be allowed to lay dormant within you; it should always be energizing you to live a life with joy, power, and hope. The power that you have been given will enable you to obey the words of Scripture. The power that is now yours will give you the courage to tell others about Christ. The power that turned the world upside down 2,000 years ago is now yours to turn your world upside down!

Show Me the Power

Many believers slog through life never tapping into the power that Peter and Paul both knew so well. The very lives of first century Christians depended upon the power of Pentecost and the indwelling of the Holy Spirit. In Bethlehem, Jesus came to live *with* us, but at Pentecost, He came to live *in* us.

If you long to live with the dynamism and vitality that you know you were created for, perhaps now would be a perfect moment to revitalize your relationship with the Holy Spirit. If you are brave enough, perhaps this prayer will renew your strength and restore your courage:

> Jesus, thank You for living in my heart. I am so grateful that You have forgiven my sins and that You have given me the promise of eternal life. Today, Jesus, I am asking for the power of the Holy Spirit to come alive in me! I am praying for every fruit that the Holy Spirit has in His garden to grow in abundance inside of me. I am asking for the same power that raised Christ from the dead to quicken the dead places in me. I am asking for the power of Pentecost to give me the power that Paul and Peter lived with. In Jesus's name I pray. And my life is available for You to deposit in me every single gift that the Holy Spirit has to offer. Amen.

Extremes

Peter has always been enthusiastic; he was filled with vitality before the resurrection and even more so after he saw the risen Savior. Peter had an ardent nature before Pentecost and after the infilling of the Holy Spirit, he became even more zealous. Peter is simply exuberant about living a life at full throttle for Christ.

Although Peter often chooses to speak in extremes, the joy of it all for me is that Peter is not exaggerating one little bit.

Seeing that His divine power has granted us everything pertaining to life and godliness.　　　　　　　　　　　　　　　—2 Peter 1:3

According to the Holy Spirit, who gave Peter the words to write in this small but weighty book of the Bible, you have been given *everything* that you need to live a life of God's approval. In order for you to live a dynamic life, God the Father didn't give you just *some* of the things required, or *most* of what was needed, or *nearly all* of the gifts that He has available. Instead, He has generously given you *everything* that you need to live a strong, noble, and *vibrant* life. He has given you *everything* that you need for every day, in every situation, and with every type of challenge.

My friend, rather than getting up in the morning and dreading your day before your feet even hit the ground, why don't you declare these words the instant that your alarm awakens you to consciousness: "Because of Christ, I have everything that I will need today to live a life of heaven's approval!"

Instead of floundering through parenting and living a life of spiritual mediocrity, try shouting this declaration over life's mundane moments: "I have been given every ounce of strength and joy that I need today to live a rare and exhilarating life!"

Rather than throwing in the towel when it comes to personal disciplines and choosing to serve others, declare this truth: "I can do all things through Christ who gives me His very own strength!"

Truth

After reminding us that God's *"divine power has granted us everything"* that we need, Peter then points out that this comes to us *"through the true knowledge of Him who called us by His own glory and excellence"* (2 Peter 1:3).

As we continue to get to know the Lord whom we serve, we will have the amazing realization that His glory calls us and His excellence restores us. As His character oozes into the humanity that defines us, we will discover that it is His glory that leaks out of us in all situations in life. As we spend time at His feet, our lives will grow in excellence and honor.

Would you pray with me today:

Jesus, I want to know You more. I want to know Your power and Your strength. I want to be the recipient of Your grace and Your glory. Jesus, this is a bold prayer, but would You use me in the same way that You used Peter and Paul? In Your powerful name I pray. Amen.

God has every bit of me.
—William Booth,
on why his life displayed such spiritual power

31

A Partner and a Partaker

I believe that in the deepest place in each one of us, at our core, our chief desire in life is to simply be like Jesus. How I long to respond like He did to difficult and cantankerous people! How I pray to teach the principles of heaven with the same power and insight that He did! How I pine to pray in spite of human pain and to see miraculous answers like Jesus did when He was on earth. How I ache to do absolutely anything just like Jesus did!

Peter now lets us in on a little secret ... that is actually not so much of a secret. I can picture the enthusiastic Peter calling me by name and asking me to draw close as he grins and his eyes sparkle. I can almost hear his rugged voice whispering to me across the ages, "Carol, if you want to be like Jesus, this is what you must do!"

These are the words that call each one of us to be a living, breathing demonstration of the character of Christ:

---

*For by these He has granted to us His **precious** and magnificent promises, so that by them you may become partakers of the divine nature,* *having escaped the corruption that is in the world by lust.*

—2 Peter 1:4

Precious Peter

It has always been a little absurd to me that Peter, the rough and tumble fisherman who was truly a *man's man*, chose *precious* as one of his recurring words.

I have a sweet southern friend who never sweats, whose makeup is always perfect, and whose pinky is always bent just so … and *her* favorite word is *precious*. In her feminine yet fragile opinion, everything is *precious*—babies, puppies, the fresh flower bouquets that adorn her home, and even a luncheon that's prepared for us. It's all utterly precious in her sugary, feminine opinion!

How in the world could Peter, the man who cut off a soldier's ear and pulled in heavy nets full of fish, ever stoop his manly self to use the word *precious?* It's incredulous, isn't it?

Peter first used this word to describe our faith:

*So that the proof of your faith, being more **precious** than gold which is perishable, even though tested by fire, may be found to result in praise and glory and honor at the revelation of Jesus Christ.*

—1 Peter 1:7

Peter then utilized this tender word to portray the blood of Jesus:

*But with **precious** blood, as of a lamb unblemished and spotless, the blood of Christ.*   *—1 Peter 1:19*

The Greek word translated as precious is *timios*, which means valuable, costly, or having a great price. *Timios* also means "held in honor, esteemed, especially dear." Peter, the unpolished disciple whose life had been refined and chiseled by his faith, knew the value of the word *precious* and he chose to use it often.

A Promise Is a Promise

Peter understood the magnificence and the honor that the promises of God hold for those who choose to believe. Peter knew there is nothing more valuable to our lifestyle than appropriating the truth of God's promises to our everyday behavior. However, in order for you to *own* the promises, you must first be aware of them.

In my daily Bible reading, whenever I come across a promise that God has made to me, I write the word *promise* in the margin beside that verse in red ink with all capital letters. Although I can't share every promise in the Bible with you that I have discovered over the course of my life, I can share a few that will help you on your journey to fill your heart with the character and nature of Christ:

But [Jesus] said, "The things that are impossible with people are possible with God."   —Luke 18:27

The Son of Man has come to seek and save that which was lost.
                                                                                 —Luke 19:10

Seek first His kingdom and His righteousness, and all these things will be added to you.   —Matthew 6:33

But if God so clothes the grass of the field, which is alive today and tomorrow is thrown into the furnace, will He not much more clothe you? You of little faith!   —Matthew 6:30

Ask, and it will be given to you; seek, and you will find; knock, and it will be opened to you. For everyone who asks receives, and he who seeks finds, and to him who knocks it will be opened.

—Matthew 7:7–8

And lo, I am with you always, even to the end of the age.

—Matthew 28:20

When you and I, who have been made in the exact image and likeness of God, apply His promises to our human lives, we begin to walk in the power and strength that He has designed for us. When I attach my life to His Word, I become more like Him and less like me.

I have found this practice of applying God's promises to my life to be especially helpful when I am in a battle. When the enemy is throwing his fiery darts toward me, I take the time to ask the Father, "What promise should I fight with? Would You give me a fighting verse, Father?"

And then, when I fight with His promises rather than with my emotions, I become a force to be reckoned with! I am armed with the Word of God, which is the sword of the Spirit.

Paul said, "All of the promises of God are yes and amen in Christ!" (See 2 Corinthians 1:20). This is an unparalleled concept in Scripture. Every time that you or I encounter a promise in the Word of God, Christ whispers in our ear, "This promise is for you! Put your name there! I am saying, 'Yes!' to this promise! It's yours!"

Just Like Jesus

What do you do with your regrets? Do you sweep them under your pillow at night along with a thousand tears? Do you decorate your life with them like Christmas lights so that the entire world can see how expansively you have blown it?

I have learned that if I do not deal with my regrets in a healthy and holy manner, they will hang around my life like yesterday's garbage and be a smelly reminder of all of the ways that I am not like Jesus.

However, if I can apply the Word of God to my mistakes and my failures, it is then that my regrets can actually become a springboard for wisdom. Regrets should never shame me, but they should create a more humble me. Regrets, when viewed under the spectrum of Scripture, enable me to grow into a godlier version of myself, a woman who is more like Jesus.

It is stunning to realize that Peter and the Holy Spirit have invited us to be *"partakers of the divine nature"* (2 Peter 1:4).

Because of Jesus, I don't have to wear my great aunt's temper or my grandfather's propensity to criticize. I get to exhibit the divine nature.

Because of the Holy Spirit, I don't have to grumble when I don't get my way or criticize someone who has been cruel to me. I get to demonstrate the divine nature.

Because of Calvary, I don't have to be filled with shame over past sins or stay up all night worrying. I am called to evidence the divine nature.

Because of the Word of God, I don't have to wonder what God's will is or wander aimlessly through life. I am a show-and-tell on planet earth of how to live life filled with God's holy and lovely nature.

One of the most glorious parts of this lifestyle is that we don't *have to* be like Jesus, but we *get to* be like Him! It is the highest honor and privilege as we walk through this life in which the world is aching for someone to give them Jesus.

The Escape Clause

As you continue to exhibit the nature of Christ out of your earthly pores, Peter and the Holy Spirit promise that you will escape *"the corruption that is in the world by lust"* (2 Peter 1:4).

Peter was obviously concerned about the world that the first-century church was encountering. He knew it would be a difficult journey for them as they dealt with persecution, separation from families, lack of resources, and even, perhaps, the threat of an early death. Now remember, because these verses are inspired by the Holy Spirit, although they were written to the early church, they were written for us as well!

Peter knew that although we walk in the victory of our faith, in the truth of Scripture, and in the power of the Holy Spirit, we would naturally face some difficulties along life's way.

However, when we determine to be the human expression of the character of Christ, it opens an escape door for us!

Paul expressed it this way:

Walk by the Spirit, and you will not carry out the desire of the flesh. For the flesh sets its desire against the Spirit, and the Spirit against the flesh; for these are in opposition to one another, so that you may not do the things that you please. —Galatians 5:16–17

You really don't want to be like *you* at your weakest. You want to be like Him! Believe me when I tell you that there's a better way to live than demanding your own way. When you submit to His will and His ways, the blessings will be eternal and the difference will be magnificent.

Would you pray with me today:

Lord Jesus, I want to be just like You! I don't want to be like me and live my life with regrets but I want Your nature and Your character to be evident in every word that I speak, every emotion I exhibit, and every action that I participate in. In Jesus's wonderful name I pray. Amen.

Don't bother to give God instructions, just report for duty.
—Corrie ten Boom

32

Quality and Quantity

Aind now, our new best friend, Peter, becomes extremely practical in his advice to anyone who longs to become a partaker of the divine nature. His coaching moves from visionary and philosophical to the nitty-gritty of how to live a life of no regrets.

As I read this list, I realize that what Peter is saying to me is that I must be intentional daily in my walk with Christ. I must determine in very specific areas of my life to choose Him and His characteristics rather than what seems easy or expedient. Saying a resounding "Yes!" to the instructions in the Word of God will always lead to a life of joy.

As we read this list together and examine the instructions found therein, I am struck by the fact that every single priority that Peter is advising us to make a vital part of our lives is actually an inner work rather than an outward action. While it is true that inner works will eventually reveal themselves outwardly in the words that we speak and the actions we demonstrate, Peter's advice is to let it begin on the inside first. Peter, my

favorite disciple, reminds me tenderly yet pointedly that the most important task of my life is not found in what I accomplish, but is most evident in
who I choose to become.

---

*Now for this very reason also, applying all diligence, in your faith
supply moral excellence, and in your moral excellence, knowledge,
and in your knowledge, self-control, and in your self-control, perseverance, and in your perseverance, godliness, and in your godliness,
brotherly kindness, and in your brotherly kindness, love.*

—2 Peter 1:5–7

I Resolve

Oh, how Peter wants us to be partakers of the divine nature! It is such
an imperative for him that he has created a list of choices to ponder on a
daily basis. Perhaps Peter is concerned that we will forget what exactly
constitutes a godly character on this side of eternity. Peter knows human
nature so well because he is human and he struggled deeply and fought
intensely to exhibit the characteristics of the Father in his life. However,
Peter experienced gargantuan strides and healthy growth, making him
a qualified coach to lead believers into embracing a disciplined and well-
honed life that will reveal the Jesus in us.

Peter presents the unarguable case that diligence is one of the most
valuable character traits that one can choose to embrace. If we are not
diligent, we will not to be able to have the tenacity to grasp the other
characteristics that are in this long but exciting list. If our goal in life is
to exhibit the divine nature of God Himself, we must partner with Him
in the production of all that is good and noble on the inside of our being.
We must make every effort to actively and relentlessly seek the character
traits that Peter invites us to produce. When your determination partners
with God's power, the godliness that will shine forth from your life will be
simply magnificent! When you resolve to take Peter's advice, the world will
recognize you as a person who has been with Jesus!

Faith

Faith is the foundation of everything else in life! Without childlike faith, the Bible says, we are unable to please God. (See Mark 10:15; Luke 18:17.) Therefore, faith is the most vital component to this exceptional lifestyle for which we were created.

Peter, and the Holy Spirit, have invited us to embrace a lively and hopeful faith. Your faith in Christ should be the petri dish for every word that you speak, every relationship you enter into, and every decision that you make. Your faith in Christ should be the DNA of who you are as a person.

Fertilizing your faith to rapid and dynamic growth always includes a lifestyle that honors Christ. *"Faith without works is dead"* (James 2:26). Your faith was never meant to be philosophical only; it was always meant to change the way you think, act, and speak.

Your faith in Christ should determine your calendar, your moral choices, and your personal disciplines. Faith is neither dead nor unresponsive! Faith awakens the shriveled soul to a lifestyle of genuine hope. Faith changes the *impossible* to the *possible*! Faith in God is the true north for a disciple of Christ.

"Have faith in God," were the words of Jesus in Mark 11:22. Jesus knew that misplaced faith would always misplace a person who was made in the image of God! Faith should be the jubilant music to which your life dances and the delectable buffet from which your soul eats. Faith is your only reliable compass in the storm and the oil that makes the mechanisms of your life work easily and smoothly.

Be diligent in your faith!

Moral Excellence

Moral excellence can also be translated as *virtue* ... and I must tell you, I have grown to love this word. Some may believe that virtue is old-fashioned, out of date, or even archaic, but I believe that virtue is a courageous word that we dare not ignore.

What you choose to do on a daily basis matters—it matters very much. How you choose to live your life sexually, mentally, physically, emotionally, and spiritually matters to the plan of God for your life. You were not created to slog through the excrement of our culture and merely imagine the possibility of living a life of unquenchable joy and unmatched purpose. You were *made for more* than this world can offer. You were created for moral excellence!

There is a difference between right and wrong, and as children of God, we must always choose right. We simply must! If the Bible says it is wrong, then it is wrong. We must not argue with the principles or instructions found in the Bible. Many people believe that God has changed with the culture, but I can assure you that *He has not changed one iota*. He is the same yesterday, today, and forever. (See Hebrews 13:8.) He has not changed His mind regarding what is sin or what is acceptable in His kingdom.

You will never be the person that God has called you to be if you are choosing to live a life of moral compromise. Your vibrant faith will always call you to honor the principles and the heart of God in all of your daily decisions.

Being a man or a woman of moral excellence is not legalism, nor is it prudish behavior. It is a certainty that God's framework for life is beautiful and exquisite. You were not made for captivity in the sewage of our culture; you were created for the finest and noblest life that has ever existed.

Moral excellence was never meant to restrain you; it was meant to liberate you!

Be diligent in your moral excellence.

Knowledge

One of the most riveting and astonishing aspects of life on earth is that we are invited to spend time with the Father and thus get to know Him better. What an uncommon delight! No matter how deep your walk with the Lord might be, there is always more to be experienced, more to examine, and more to learn. If we were to spend every second of every day for the rest of our lives just focused on God and on who He is, we would still never learn everything that there is to know about Him! We are finite and He is infinite; we are human and He is divine. We are the created and He is the Creator; we are sinners and He is our loving Savior.

You and I will never become an expert in the riches of God, but we will always be invited to a lifetime of acquainting ourselves with Him. We are summoned to know Him daily and to enjoy Him continuously.

The Lord's lovingkindnesses indeed never cease, for His compassions never fail. They are new every morning; great is Your faithfulness. —Lamentations 3:22–23

The enemy does not want you to know the God whom you serve and will do everything possible to keep you from knowing the Father. He does not want you to become acquainted with the glory and goodness that belongs only to the Father. That wretched deceiver will cause you to be too busy to read your Bible or convince you that you are too weary to go to church. The enemy of your soul uses distraction to keep you from developing a vibrant prayer life and he employs confusion to lead you away from your faith. My friend, remind yourself daily that knowing Jesus and loving the Father is the best part of your life. Absolutely nothing else compares to the fulfillment that you experience when you spend your life knowing Him in more intimate and exciting ways every day you are alive.

Be diligent in getting to know the Father!

Self-Control

Self-control is a compound word that often makes us cringe. To some people, the word *self-control* is much like fingernails on the chalkboard of life, isn't it? If you're tempted right now to skim over this portion, don't do it! I have had the same thoughts about self-control that you might have, but I've learned that self-control will indeed make me more like Jesus—and I want all of Him that I can get!

We all know that we need a greater degree of self-control, but we also all hate to admit it! Somehow, our soul has led us to believe that self-control kills the pleasures of life. While it is true that self-control is not always fun, when you have made diligence the foundation in your quest to exhibit the divine nature, you know intrinsically that you have the tools to make the right choices in life. So, rather than dread the idea of self-control, let's re-examine it and see how it can enhance our walk of faith.

At its root, the Greek word that is used for self-control refers to mastery over sinful human desires in every area of life. An astounding realization is that *self-control* really does not change me intrinsically in the long run. I need to allow God to have full control over everything that goes into my mouth and that comes out of my mouth. I need to allow God to control the hours of my days and what I do with those days. I must allow God to control my thought life and my spending habits. I must partner with the Holy Spirit to live a life of godly, supernatural control. My self-control is only effective to the degree that I allow God to control me!

Self-control is a fruit of the Holy Spirit. Oh, how I need the Holy Spirit to help me control my eating, spending, talking, thinking, and choosing! Without the power of the Holy Spirit, my self-control would result in selfish opinions, selfish behaviors, and self-seeking habits.

Be diligent in allowing God to control the personal disciplines of your life.

Perseverance

It has always been so intriguing to me that Peter names *perseverance* immediately after self-control in his list of godly behaviors. (See 2 Peter 1:5–7.) I readily admit that if I hope to partner with the Holy Spirit in controlling my bent to overindulge in fleshly desires, I must persevere in it! I must decide ahead of time not to throw in that infamous towel or give up easily.

Perseverance, in some translations, is cited as *patient endurance*. As a woman of God, I must have the character trait to patiently endure difficult days, challenging people, and times of lack, as well as the stamina to march forward in the tough stuff of life. I am able to patiently endure when I am utterly convinced that God is good and that He will have the final say in all of my life's situations.

"Someone needs to see you suffer well." These are the words of Elisabeth Elliot, whose first husband was murdered on the mission field and whose second husband died a painful death from cancer. Perseverance is the decision to suffer well; perseverance is the decision not to complain about your life but to sing persistently and joyfully instead.

Perseverance is refusing to give up emotionally when the fires are fierce and the storms are unrelenting. Perseverance is the decision to set your gaze toward the Father, to allow the Word of God to come alive in your heart, and to march forward in faith and in hope.

Perseverance never complains, but stares unflinchingly at the goodness of God.

Be diligent to persevere.

Godliness

Godliness is the one attribute that sets a believer in Christ apart from the merely good behavior that the world espouses. We are not being good for the sake of goodness, but we are entwining the character of God Himself in our emotional and spiritual makeup. You are not an earthly angel filled with human virtue who never does anything wrong, but you *are* the consummate demonstration of what people can be when they choose to be like Jesus! How magnificent is that?!

I must be more aware of the heart of the Father than I am of my own preferences in life. The guiding principle of my life must be a pervasive and unrelenting drive to simply be like Jesus, every day in every way. I don't want to be like me—I deeply desire to be like Him.

I ache to show the world who the Father is by the words that I speak, the choices that I make, and the love that I share. I have decided that at the end of my life, I simply want people to remember that I was a woman who sought diligently and humbly to be like Jesus.

The character of God is within me because I have invited Jesus to live in my heart. Godliness is the choice to allow the character of God to be seen in me. Godliness is the decision to let Jesus leak out of me. Godliness is inviting the Father to reveal Himself to others through me.

The world needs many things today, but I believe what it needs most desperately is more good people who dare to live godly lives. When the culture tastes the goodness of God in your life, it will inevitably hunger for more.

Be diligent in your godliness.

Brotherly Kindness and Love

One of the amazing opportunities that we are given as believers is that we are invited to love one another as brothers and sisters in Christ. It's not a *have-to* but it is a *get-to*. I have learned to embrace this privilege not as a harsh mandate but rather as an exciting distinction. As the sons and daughters of the God whose very character is identified as Love, we get to love and demonstrate practical kindness to those whom the world would reject or classify as *unlovable*.

Love is never revealed without kindness and even emergent kindness will often grow into love. When we choose to respond in a kind manner, we become a kinder person. When we choose to love the dysfunctional and the difficult, we become more like our Father.

This is not the first time that Peter called the early church—and therefore you and me—to a lifestyle of exuberant and unrestricted love. Peter declares that one of the most important aspects of our entire lives is the manner in which we love each other.

> *Above all, keep fervent in your love for one another, because love covers a multitude of sins.* —1 Peter 4:8

Love should never be passive, but always dynamic; love should never be mediocre, but always enthusiastic! Who do you need to love today? Who have you been passive toward who needs your generous kindness and love?

Peter realized what you and I often ignore: love fills us rather than drains us. Kindness makes our lives larger not smaller. When we give love and kindness to others, *we* are direct beneficiaries of that choice. Love and kindness always enhance the lifestyle of the giver. Always.

Be diligent to be enthusiastically kind and show unconditional love!

Would you pray with me today:

Lord Jesus, would You do an inner work in me today? Would You help me to become the person that You created me to become? Lord, would You lay the names and faces of people who need more love from me on my heart right now? Would You give me creative ideas so that I can demonstrate true kindness to them? Lord, fan the flames of love and kindness in me today. In Jesus's loving name I pray. Amen.

The greatest thing a man or a woman can do for his or her Heavenly Father is to be kind to some of His other children.
—Henry Drummond

33

Put Your Glasses On

Do you wear glasses or contacts? I have worn very strong eyeglasses since I was in third grade. Early in the school year, my vivacious and perceptive teacher sent a note home from school, encouraging my parents to have my eyes checked. She noticed that I was unable to see what was written on the board and I was holding my books very close to my face while reading.

My aghast and somewhat embarrassed mother took me to the family eye doctor and sure enough, glasses would solve many of my reading and learning issues. The glasses were ordered—cute blue frames with silver butterflies on the corners—and we waited for their arrival.

I'll never forget the sensation as I walked out of the optometrist's office, holding my mother's hand and exclaiming, "Mom! I can see the steps! I know where to put my feet!"

In the following days, I read every road sign, read the newspaper to my dad, read the Bible at family devotions, and blurted out answers in the classroom. My life had been changed! I could see!

The Perceptive Peter

Peter is also concerned about our vision. But unlike my third grade teacher, who was merely concerned about my physical eyesight, Peter addresses our *spiritual* perception. He knows that if we don't order our lives under the principles that he has presented, we will have a problem seeing ourselves and our lives the way God does.

Peter doesn't want us to be blind, nearly blind, or to only see what is in front of our faces. Peter is convinced that if we can exhibit the qualities that he has listed, we will have spiritual vision that will enhance our lives.

In addition, Peter deeply desires that we have the capacity to serve Christ for the long haul of life and he is poignantly aware that it will require some difficult yet beautiful choices in our daily walk.

For if these qualities are yours and are increasing, they render you neither useless nor unfruitful in the true knowledge of our Lord Jesus Christ. For he who lacks these qualities is blind or shortsighted, having forgotten his purification from his former sins.

—2 Peter 1:8–9

If I choose laziness over diligence, I become shortsighted and falsely suppose that what I do on a daily basis doesn't actually matter in the duration of my life. Spiritual blindness might convince me that choosing what is expedient is the easiest and best choice rather than choosing to live with focused discipline.

If I choose compromise over moral excellence, I am blind to the consequences. If I choose to ignore God over getting to know Him fully, I am not gazing into my future but only looking at this passing moment.

When I was at a crossroads of choosing well or not, my father often told me, "Carol, it might not look like it pays to serve Jesus in the short-run of life, but in the long haul, it always makes a difference. When you choose Jesus today, you are choosing a brilliant future tomorrow."

Perpetually Growing

Isn't it also interesting to note that Peter asserts that we must not allow these characteristics to grow stagnant inside of us? The truth that Peter is promoting in this particular passage is the unalterable fact that a person will never become a bona fide expert at diligence, faith, moral excellence, knowing God, self-control, perseverance, godliness, kindness, or love. There is always more to learn.

What Peter has vividly presented in this passage are the required steps for a believer in Christ to grow in faith and in maturity. Peter has enthusiastically reminded us that God always has something more for us—something extraordinary and breathtakingly beautiful!

I am challenged by the words and by the call of Peter! I resolve today to cultivate the agriculture of the kingdom of God in my life. I deeply long for God to use me; therefore, I will accommodate His glorious plans for my life.

- I will be a person of undeniable faith and stellar moral excellence.

- I will spend my life getting to know God better and allowing Him to control my passions and desires.

- I will persevere! I will refuse to ever give up! I will choose to emulate God in my actions, my words, and my emotions.

- I will be kind to everyone regardless of how I am treated and I will become a vessel through which God can pour out His unconditional love.

Would you pray with me today:

Lord Jesus, thank You that I don't have to go through life being blind or shortsighted in my choices. Today I choose You and all that You are! I long for You to use me in Your kingdom so I ask for divine appointments today. Order my steps in such a way that my path will cross the paths of others who need You. In Jesus's name I pray. Amen.

We never grow closer to God when we just live life. It takes deliberate pursuit and attentiveness.
—Francis Chan

34

No More Stumbling

Now we will stumble upon the exciting *why* of these matchless verses of Scripture that bear Peter's name. There was a reason why he reminded us of the importance of getting to know God better every day, and reminded us that we are called by glory and excellence. There was a reason why Peter reminded us of the valuable promises that are ours in Christ, and why Peter invited us to become partakers of the divine nature.

This, then, is the obvious *why*:

---

*Therefore, brethren, be all the more diligent to make certain about His calling and choosing you; for as long as you practice these things, you will never **stumble**.* —2 Peter 1:10

Do you see the promise nestled deeply in the words of this verse? Peter's goal was to present the case that if we follow his instructions, which were inspired by the Holy Spirit, we will no longer stumble! We no longer have to tell little white lies or yell at our kids. We no longer have to give our spouse the silent treatment or ignore our mother's phone calls. We no longer have to drown our sorrows in eating or shopping. We no longer have to gossip or spew venom on people. We can live a life where we never stumble again!

You might understandably wonder, *Is that even possible?* But Peter and the Holy Spirit assure us that this type of life is not merely a vague possibility, but an irrefutable probability when we live by the verses that I like to call the *Peter Principles*.

Necessary Review

Because this promised lifestyle is so extraordinary, let's review one more time the steps that it will take to live a life of no more stumbling. These are valuable life principles and I absolutely do not want you to overlook their importance in your daily life and in building your legacy:

- Grace and peace are multiplied to you when you simply take the time to get to know the Lord intimately.

- Then … you are invited to tap into His divine power, which will enable you to live a life of strength and holiness.

- Then … you decide to value His promises and apply them to your daily life.

- Then … your nature actually begins to change as you become more like Him.

- Then … the world no longer has the ability to entice you into its compromises.

- Then … you become more certain of His calling and choosing of you.

- Then … you never stumble!

Don't Trip!

You can be certain, my friend, that the Creator of the universe has truly called you by your name—remember, it's Beloved—and has chosen you to be part of His grand plan. You can believe this one unquestionable truth with no doubts and with ebullient faith! If there is one undeniable fact upon which you can build a solid life it is that you are called and chosen by the One who knows you best and loves you the most! My heart is filled with song even as I type these thrilling words that are laced with eternal truth.

You are called. You are chosen. Now you must determine personally to what degree you will live for Christ and His kingdom. You choose whether to choose Him or not every day in a thousand ways both big and small. You elect exactly what the depth of your walk in Christ will be by whether or not you embrace the virtues of godly living that Peter has invited you to drench yourself in.

God has decided that you are His by His own initiative. Now, it remains up to you to decide how much of God you want. He wants all of you.

Do you want all of Him?

If you choose the Lord and His ways above your own preferences and desires, you will never stumble. You will live a life of sheer beauty and obvious joy when all that you are bows in worship to all that He is.

The word *stumble* in 2 Peter 1:10 is the Greek word *patio*, which can also be translated as *to fail*. Isn't it wonderful to realize that in life, we don't have to fail, but we can soar through situations sheltered by His love and care? The Holy Spirit has made a way for you to make it through life with as little injury as possible!

Unfortunately, you can insist that you know better than the Father and spew verbal vomit all over people; you can also selfishly demand your own way and refuse to forgive those who have wronged you. If you choose to live life your own way based on compromise, smug behavior, and fleshly desires, you will stumble and fall often. You will bang up your heart and the hearts of those around you. You will suffer from soul abrasions, mind contusions, and self-inflicted wounds.

Will you choose to fall or will you choose to stand? Will you choose to stumble or will you walk confidently through this life you have been given?

My Poor Knees

I was not very coordinated as a child although I grew into a rather competent athlete in my high school years. Even though I diligently worked at it, I didn't learn how to ride a bicycle until I was nearly in the fourth grade.

At the end of third grade, I had saved enough money to invest in my very own, brand new, pink and white Schwinn bike. My father drove me to Batavia, the seat of Genesee County, New York, home to the only bicycle store in our area. I'd had my eye on this beautiful bike for months and couldn't believe that now it would be mine!

There was only one formidable impediment to my relationship with this sparkling thirty-six-inch piece of wonder: I didn't know how to ride a bike yet! My father promised that he would help me and every day, when he arrived home from work, he held the bike while I climbed on. Then he ran down the slope of our driveway while holding onto the seat. I would be screaming, "Daddy! Don't let go of me! Don't let go!"

My patient father cheerfully promised, "Honey, I won't let go of you until you get your balance." And he didn't. My dad was as good as his word.

Every evening, my father would remind me to look up as I rode my bike and to choose an object in the distance to focus on rather than looking down at my rotating feet. I can remember him saying, "Carol, you will never learn balance until you stop being afraid of falling. Choose something to look at in front of you and keep your eyes set on that one thing."

I was so determined to ride this incredible bike for which I had scrimped and saved that finally, I just decided that I would do it on my own. I didn't wait for my dad to get home from work, but ventured across the street to a vacant parking lot. Around and around I went, falling time after time after time. My knees were battered and bruised, but I was stubborn in my persistence to ride my bike. I simply couldn't figure out how to balance; I would wobble back and forth until I finally hit the pavement.

By the end of my first week of riding and falling, my knees had taken such a beating that there was pus dripping down my legs. In the mornings when I awoke, my pajama legs would be stuck to my knees. The only way to take my pajamas off was to soak in the tub first and then gently remove the fabric from the infected wounds.

Early one morning, as my dad was tenderly nursing my damaged knees, he began to pray over me, "Lord, would You help Carol learn how to ride her bike? She needs Your strength and balance in her life. Protect her, Lord."

From that day on, I improved in my cycling ability. I was able to catch myself before I fell and I learned the secret of keeping my eyes set on an object in the distance in order to maintain my balance. It wasn't long before my dad was cheering for me as I took to the open road! My knees finally healed and my confidence was restored.

Although decades removed from falling off my bike, my knees are still scarred to this very day ... but they no longer cause me pain. I learned how to balance my bicycle when I listened to the voice of my earthly father and I have learned how to balance in life when I was diligent in my attempts to please my heavenly Father.

Set Your Gaze

If you long to go through life free from wounds and pain, then you will set your eyes on the Father and you will listen to His voice. If today you bear the scars of past foolish decisions, remind yourself that today is a new day to obey! Set your eyes on the plans and principles that have been written just for you in the Word of God and never take your eyes off of His truth. Be diligent in your attempts to please Him and you will discover, just as I did as a child, that balance is all about focus. I choose to focus on Him and to hear His voice above all others. I choose.

Would you pray with me today:

Dear Lord, I love You so much. Thank You for being such a good, good Father. I pray that You will help me be diligent in my walk of faith and that You will protect me from pain and from injury. Thank You, Dad, for calling me and for choosing me. I love being Your daughter! In Jesus's name I pray. Amen.

When we are calling to God to turn the eye of His favor towards us, He is calling to us to turn the eye of our obedience towards Him.

—Matthew Henry

PART EIGHT

One Final Invitation

35

The Grand Canyon

The book of Ephesians is expansive and intimate, beautiful and challenging. At times, I have called Ephesians *the Grand Canyon of the Bible*. In my studies, I have often pictured myself standing on the edge of this epistle and gazing into its depths. I knew in those moments that I could enjoy the magnificence of Ephesians, go diving into it, climb to the top of it, and take a deep breath … but that there was no human way that I could ever experience every massive thought or each cherished word in this epic book written by none other than Paul.

Ephesians is so rich, so grand, and so multifaceted that in our own human thinking or limited mental ability, we will never be able to embrace every cell of its structure. However, let's try to at least capture the essence of one of its streams of abundant living. Let's go digging for gold into the storehouse that is Ephesians and discover treasures from heaven upon its pages. You are about to tap into the mother lode of vibrant living!

The portion of Ephesians that we are going to linger over holds a cache of wealth that may trigger, all at once, beads of sweat, incredulity, and undeserved delight. Ephesians is both practical and purposeful in our unending quest to live a life of unrivaled joy and beauty. And I pray that it will enable us to harvest all that is grand and eternal in this life that we have been called to cultivate by the Creator of the universe.

You Belong to Me

We were never placed on planet earth to live separate and apart from others; the plan of the Father, from the garden of Eden forward, was for us, as His dear children, to discover the satisfaction and wonder of human relationships. It is in partnering with others in the family, in the church, in a neighborhood, or in the workplace that we explore the healthy kinship that was meant to enlarge us.

If there is one location that the enemy diligently endeavors to saturate with grief, rejection, and annoyance, it is in human relationships. And if there is one place that the Lord desires to bless with fulfillment, contentment, and unconditional love, it is in human relationships.

Therefore, laying aside falsehood, speak truth each one of you with his neighbor, for we are members of one another.

—Ephesians 4:25

The injunction is quite clear that all relationships should only be built on the foundational issue of truth. You will never cultivate lasting or healthy friendships if you choose to deceive the people in your life. Paul says you must completely remove all types of sordid duplicity from your life. Never again, in this gorgeous new life that you are called to live, should you choose to fib, to exaggerate, or to speak an untruth. Politicians might be fraudulent, family members might fabricate, and your boss might be a hypocrite, but it is not who *you* are. *You* are a truth-telling, honest, genuine representation of the heart of the Father! It's who you are at your core.

There is only one entity that tricks you into a life of fraud and he is the father of all lies. When you choose, by your own free will, to give an answer of duplicity or to deceive someone in order to make yourself look better, you are listening to and therefore partnering with the enemy of this splendid life that you have been called to create.

However, let me also remind you that neither should you be a raw mountain of truth ready to explode your coarse perspective over an unsuspecting person! As carriers of God's divine nature, we should be on the journey of learning to combine love, wisdom, and truth together in a beautiful and fragrant bouquet.

We belong to each other and we should treat one another as we desire to be treated ourselves. I have realized over the course of my life that my goal is to speak to other people the way that I want people to speak to my children. I do hope that people will tell my children the truth, but I want them to be both wise and kind in their honest approach.

Boundaries and Sunsets

I once embarked on a very specific Bible study that targeted precisely what God's Word teaches us about human emotions. One of my interesting discoveries was that there are some human emotions that are allowable according to Scripture while others are not. For instance, as children of the Father, we are not allowed to worry or embrace fear and anxiety. Some human emotions are permitted ... within biblical boundaries. One such emotion is anger.

Be angry, and yet do not sin; do not let the sun go down on your anger, and do not give the devil an opportunity.
—Ephesians 4:26–27

Anger is not forbidden, but we are given very specific boundaries concerning this volatile emotion. We are only allowed to be angry, at the most, for twenty-three hours and fifty-nine minutes. When the sun begins to set in the western skies, you must let your anger go and be done with it. You must never bring it back up again.

One devastating reality is that many of us have brought anger from ten or twenty years ago into the present and it has ruined the glory that was meant to be ours today. Anger is an out-of-control weed and it will spread bitterness in our unsuspecting lives. We mistakenly believe that we have a *right* or a *reason* to be angry ... but the Bible tells us to let it go at the end of the day.

God desires for His children to be healthy emotionally and the only way for this to happen is if you choose to forgive the one who caused your anger—quickly, thoroughly, and before the next day dawns.

The word *anger* in this verse is a Greek compound word that paints the picture of a person who welcomes anger as a close companion, even embracing it. This person actually has the audacity to build a relationship with anger and then nourishes it and holds it close to his or her heart. Anger personified becomes this person's constant companion throughout life.

The Father knows what kind of long-term damage anger can do to your heart. He always knows best and He's begging you to let it go.

If your human opinion means more to you than God's perspective, you will stumble and fall. You will live a life that is void of vibrancy and purpose. Joy will become an impossible dream if the anger that has engulfed you will not bow to the principles of Scripture.

Be done with anger. Do not welcome anger as a friend and certainly don't take it to bed with you!

When we carry the load of anger from yesterday into today, we actually offer the devil an opportunity to do an unseen and vicious work in our lives. Believe me, my friend, the enemy will take full advantage of your relationship with anger and will make sure that anger's twin brothers, bitterness and strife, will also make themselves at home in your life. The devil smirks with evil glee when he observes that you have brought the anger of a decade ago into the reality of your today because he knows that your heart will be a fertile field for bitterness and depression.

The enemy wants to keep you embroiled in anger and will do anything to keep it simmering on the back burner of your heart. He will shoot flaming arrows into your thought life and might even cause others to gossip in your presence as a reminder of the situation that caused your fiery indignation.

The father of lies will deceive you into believing that you have a *right* to be angry. But you, my vibrant friend, do not have the right to embrace anger as a lifelong companion. You, who have been forgiven of much, must become an expert at forgiveness. Craig and I have resolved in our marriage that the first one to forgive is the one who wins. (And because I love to win so much, I make it a habit to fully forgive this nearly perfect man of mine!)

The devil is prowling around looking for some unsuspecting yet angry Christian to devour in the darkness of the night. That's the enemy's favorite time to pounce on us and that is the very reason why the Holy Spirit has advised us not to let the sun go down on our anger. The Father is inviting you today to live an anger-free life that is at once glorious and fruitful! We serve a loving God who leads by example and has forgiven you of your sins quickly and completely. The noble and remarkable life of your dreams is generously available with your choice to forgive.

Would you pray with me today:

Jesus, today I declare that I will let anger go! I refuse to allow anger to become a constant companion in my life. Instead, I choose to forgive those who have treated me in an unkind manner. Thank You for the example that You have given to me to be an instant forgiver. I want to be just like You, Dad ... just like You. In Jesus's name I pray. Amen.

Allowing anger to seethe on the back burner will lead to a
very large lid blowing off a very hot pot.
—Chuck Swindoll

36

Practical Persistence

Hasn't it been interesting to realize how often the Holy Spirit repeats Himself in the New Testament? We have heard—more than once—to be kind and love each other fully. The Holy Spirit has reminded us repeatedly to live a life of peace and to resist worry. We have been coached several times to be gentle in our dealings with others and to live a life of thanksgiving. I wonder why the Holy Spirit determined it was necessary to tell us the same things over and over again?

I believe the Holy Spirit gave us this vital reiteration of instruction because He knew that human beings are sometimes slow learners. As a mother, I know that I have had to remind my children to brush their teeth nearly every morning for eighteen years! I have had to reinforce my explicit instructions to my kids to make their beds and to be kind to their siblings at least a thousand times! The Holy Spirit, in His ever-so-patient ways, has taken the time and the opportunity to remind us of these foundational issues often in Scripture … and for that I am grateful, aren't you?

Although these verses in the *Grand Canyon* of Ephesians might seem like an irritating echo of what was stated earlier, the repetition is there for a reason—and the reason is you!

Don't Ignore It!

Honestly, you might wonder what the next verse has to do with your humble yet fulfilling life, yet this verse holds practical truth for all of us, regardless of our criminal record!

He who steals must steal no longer; but rather he must labor, performing with his own hands what is good, so that he will have something to share with one who has need. —Ephesians 4:28

Now, before you think that you need to have committed some crime in order for the above verse to apply to your life, let me set the record straight. The truth is that we are *all* thieves. Perhaps we have only *thought* about taking something that does not belong to us, but that is still a type of theft that the Bible calls *covetousness*.

Have you ever thought about someone else's spouse more than you have thought about your own? That is stealing.

Have you ever fantasized about an old boyfriend or girlfriend? That is stealing.

Have you ever desired someone else's body or weight? That is stealing.

Have you ever cheated on your taxes? That is stealing.

Have you ever had a cashier give you too much change that you kept instead of giving it back? That is stealing.

The Lord is inviting us to cultivate a glorious lifestyle that is free from jealousy, coveting, and even mentally embezzling what does not belong to us. If something does not belong to you, then don't abscond with it—either mentally, emotionally, or tangibly.

Work Hard

Paul is investigating a cavern that's perhaps hidden in all of our lives in this particular verse as he continues to coach us to work hard. A dedicated work ethic is a virtue that is often overlooked in today's world of instant gratification, but it is one of the most valuable characteristics parents can develop and encourage in their children.

When my two older sons were about ten and twelve years old, my extremely phlegmatic father-in-law took me aside one day and said quietly, "Carol, you are an incredible mother, but you need to teach your sons to work hard. I can help you with that if you want me to."

Well, of course I wanted his help! From that conversation forward, every Monday, my sweet father-in-law came and picked up the boys early in the morning and engaged them in his carpentry business. Since my boys were homeschooled at the time, we had the freedom to do this and I know that it has helped to shape the men that they have become. They learned how to frame a building and put up drywall; they also learned how to do basic electrical work and plumbing. If there were no tasks to do at his carpentry business, then their grandfather took them to mow someone's yard or weed a garden.

My husband's godly father knew the value of Ephesians 4:28 and he had the capacity to change his grandsons' futures by teaching them the principle of this verse. I have always been so grateful that "Pa" interfered in my mothering and saw something that I was unable to see.

Whatever you do, do your work heartily, as for the Lord rather than for men, knowing that from the Lord you will receive the reward of the inheritance. It is the Lord Christ whom you serve.
—Colossians 3:23–24

My practical, no-nonsense dad always used to tell me, "Carol, hard work never hurt anyone!" He saw in me, his little girl, a fragility that leaned toward melancholy. My dad, who was raised on a farm and never worked less than two jobs at a time, wanted me to understand, even with my sensitive nature, that *work is part of life*. In fact, work is a wonderful and fulfilling part of life.

When you're exhausted and spent from a long day of work, one of the most satisfying feelings in the world occurs as you lay your head down on your pillow at night. No matter what your work entailed—cleaning, leading, fixing, weeding, organizing, repairing, dusting, counseling, nurturing, or any number of accomplishments—if you have worked with your mind set on God, you can rest knowing that you had a productive and God-honoring day.

Work hard but work with joy! Work diligently but work with generosity! Work heartily and remind yourself often that you are working to honor the Lord!

Share

At the end of this painfully practical verse, Paul finally gets to the purpose of living an honest and industrious life: due to your diligence, you are now able to share with others what you have earned through your integrity. Honesty becomes noble when you give generously to others. Conscientious work becomes exponentially more purposeful when you are laboring to give to missionaries, to the church, and to kingdom expansion.

Generosity is an exciting and incomparable aspect of our ability to live a life of joy and purpose. You will never live the life of your dreams by hoarding or with selfish behavior. When you splash lavishly in the virtue of generosity, you will discover the reason for which you were made!

Instruct those who are rich in this present world not to be conceited or to fix their hope on the uncertainty of riches, but on God, who richly supplies us with all things to enjoy. Instruct them to do good, to be rich in good works, to be generous and ready to share, storing up for themselves the treasure of a good foundation for the future, so that they may take hold of that which is life indeed.

—1 Timothy 6:17–19

A Bigger Shovel

My father used to speak often of a man by the name of Robert Gilmour LeTourneau and his impact on the world. A few years ago, I studied this extraordinary man who truly had learned the secret of living with a generous heart. I was absolutely enthralled by his commitment to benevolence; since then, I have never approached finances or giving to the kingdom in the same way. I pray that his story touches your life just as it did mine.

As a boy growing up in the latter part of the nineteenth century, Bob was described as restless, inquisitive, energetic, stubborn … and fanatically determined to amount to absolutely nothing. His temperament strongly clashed with that of his unrelenting father's and it seemed that Bob's back got stiffer and stiffer the older he became. A big hulk of a boy, Bob came to violently hate school; he wanted to break out the school windows and kick out the walls.

To the chagrin of his Christian parents, Bob left home at the age of fourteen and became an apprentice at an ironworks. Bob studied mechanics from a correspondence course that had been given to him, although he never completed any assignments. Always ready to travel, he moved to California, where he learned welding and became familiar with the application of electricity.

However, Bob's temperament continued to get him into trouble wherever he moved. After a foundry superintendent called him a "back-talk smart aleck," Bob became homeless on the streets of Portland, Oregon. At age seventeen, this strong-willed man-child found himself big, broke, unemployed, and unemployable.

Bob turned his heart away from pride and self and turned his heart toward the God of his parents. When Bob humbled himself and finally asked God for help, he realized God had been on his side all along. It was at the crucial moment of turning his entire life over to the God of creation that Bob found that God's hand had given him special talents and abilities that could not be measured in a classroom, but in the creativity of foundries, factories, and patents.

Robert LeTourneau was the inventor of the electric wheel and at his death, he held the patents for nearly three hundred other inventions. During World War II, this genius, who grew up floundering for purpose and fulfillment, produced 70 percent of the world's earth-moving machines and always spoke of God as his chairman of the board. Robert gave 90 percent of his salary and company profits to missions, Christian education, and the church, and he lived only on the remaining 10 percent. The formerly homeless and hungry teenager, now a grown man world-renowned in the business world, said the money came in faster than he was able to give it away. LeTourneau was convinced he would never be able to out-give God, although he spent the rest of his life trying to do just that.

"I shovel it out," he would say, "and God shovels it back, but God has a bigger shovel than I do!"

The teenager who roamed from job to job on the streets of the West Coast became an adult millionaire and philanthropist. As his life verse, he chose:

Seek ye first the kingdom of God, and his righteousness; and all these things shall be added unto you.   —Matthew 6:33 KJV

Would you pray with me today:

Lord Jesus, forgive me for the times that I have taken what was not rightfully mine. I need Your strength to live a life of honesty and integrity. Lord, would You increase my work ethic? Would You help me to rediscover the delight that is found in working heartily for You? And most of all, Father, I want to be a giver. I want to be generous in my support of others. In the wonderful name of Jesus I pray. Amen.

By working for the Lord and putting my trust in Him,
I find recompense without measure and above any
possible personal material reward.
— Robert G. LeTourneau

37

Grace Talk

One of the most daunting deterrents in your quest to experience a life of unmatched vibrancy is no one other than you! Often it is *self* that gets in the way of embracing every day as if it is a miracle, every person as if he or she is a gift, and every moment as a new opportunity for significance.

I know that I can only speak for myself, not for you, but I take full responsibility for all of those times when I have removed kindness from my list of appropriate responses and for choosing to hang onto past pain rather than releasing it. Paul has dynamic advice for those of us who admit our own weakness when it comes to the treatment of others. It is simple advice and uncomplicated wisdom that comes from the heart of the Father through the pen of Paul.

Do's and Don'ts

The verse that we are about to dig into is a "wow!" verse for me. Perhaps it speaks to me so clearly because it tackles an uncomfortable issue that I have relentlessly battled over the years.

*Let no **unwholesome word** proceed from your mouth, but only such a word as is good for edification according to the need of the moment, so that it will give grace to those who hear.*

—Ephesians 4:29

Paul and the Holy Spirit have teamed up to help us with that muscular little organ that lies between our pearly whites. The injunction is this, "Don't ever, not even one time, allow an unwholesome word to come out of your mouth. Don't do it! You'll regret it! You were made for more than this!"

The phrase *"unwholesome word"* can also be translated as *corrupt communication*, which covers a multitude of issues. *Corrupt communication* could include gossip, name-calling, lies, and negative talk. It could also refer to the intensity or volume with which a phrase is spoken and the heart from which it comes. Have you seen yourself in this picture yet?

The word that Paul chose to describe this type of communication was descriptive of stinking meat so vile that it was filled with maggots. Paul is reminding us that there is a type of communication just that sickening.

I appreciate Paul's simplicity of instruction in this verse, so allow me to reiterate what Paul said simply and in language that you will certainly understand.

+ I don't get to say one critical thing … not ever.

+ I do get to speak in a wholesome manner … all the time.

+ I don't get to gossip … not ever.

+ I do get to encourage others … all the time.

+ I don't get to lambaste someone with whom I disagree … not ever.

+ I do get to thoughtfully listen and find a branch of conversational peace … all the time.

+ I don't get to tell my side of the story in order to make myself look better … not ever.

+ I do get to give a good report about what others have contributed ... all the time.

+ I don't get to whine and complain ... not ever.

+ I only get to speak grace-filled words ... all the time.

Could I just tack on one more personal note when it comes to this kind of conversational freedom? I have learned that *nine times out of ten* is not the goal in meeting Paul's assignment, nor is ninety-nine times out of a hundred good enough. This grace-filled language must be so much a part of who I am that I would never dream of speaking any other way. I must edify and encourage others all the time, every time, always and in every way possible. There is no escape clause when it comes to how we talk to others who have been made in the image of the Father.

I have learned to ask myself four vital questions before a phrase is allowed to escape from my mouth:

1. Is this true?

2. Is this wholesome?

3. Is this edifying?

4. Does it bring grace to the hearer?

Grace-Speak in the Home

Have I told you yet that I am the mother to five perfectly wonderful young adults? I gave birth to them over the course of nearly fourteen years and so when the oldest was learning how to drive a car, the youngest was not yet potty-trained. It was an exuberant, noisy, and lovely existence when my children all lived in the too-small family home.

As you can imagine, with boys and girls, toddlers and teens, introverts and extroverts, sometimes our home sounded like a war zone of emotions and opinions. In those hours, my children would know exactly what I was going to say when their voices were raised and their words were fractious: "In this home, we build. We don't tear down. Use your words as words of building, encouragement, and grace. Do not use your words to criticize, complain, or do damage."

The word *edification* actually can be defined as *to build up*. The Father has given you words for one purpose and one purpose alone: to build up those in your life. Do not use your words as a force of destruction, or to maim others emotionally. We are a family who only builds; we never destroy! Paul is reminding us of the family motto: "In this home, we build. We don't tear down."

Grief and the Holy Spirit

Directly following the verse about using our words only as tools of encouragement and grace, the Holy Spirit began to speak with Paul about an uncomfortable subject.

"Brother Paul," the Holy Spirit might have said, "when the children of God tear one another apart with their words and criticize one another and complain to each other, it grieves my heart. I have sealed the children of God for the day of redemption and you can be sure that they are going to heaven someday. However, while they are still sucking in the oxygen of planet earth, their unkind words and their ungracious tones grieve me. All the time—it grieves me."

Although you might consider this to be conjecture on my part, we can be sure that the heart of the Holy Spirit was intent on communicating His deep sadness over the way that we speak to one another.

Do not grieve the Holy Spirit of God, by whom you were sealed for the day of redemption. —Ephesians 4:30

Oftentimes in the evangelical church or in charismatic circles, the phrase *grieve the Holy Spirit* is applied to behavior in church services. Sometimes, we might believe that talking in church while the pastor is preaching is *grieving the Holy Spirit*. Some might think that using certain types of instruments or lights in the sanctuary *grieves the Holy Spirit*. However, that is not the context in which the phrase is used.

When this verse is studied in context, we see that it has been strategically and divinely placed between two verses that deal with human relationships and how we, as believers in Christ, are expected to treat one another and speak to one another. Thus, you can be assured, when you speak unkindly to someone, it grieves the Holy Spirit. When you lash out in anger or impatience, it grieves the Holy Spirit.

The word that the Holy Spirit whispered into Paul's ear to use concerning this situation is *grieve.* It is only possible to grieve someone who loves you dearly. Isn't it wonderful to know that you are loved dearly by the Holy Spirit? He longs to have a personal and precious relationship with you.

Oh! I don't want to be guilty of grieving someone who loves me dearly, do you? I long for my life to be a fragrant aroma not a vile odor to the Holy Spirit. I have learned that pleasing the Holy Spirit is more than just reading my Bible, giving my tithe, or spending time on my knees in prayer. The Holy Spirit is pleased with my life when I speak words of grace even in contentious situations.

Would you pray with me today:

Lord Jesus, I want to bring pleasure to Your heart especially in my relationships with others. I repent right now for the words that I have spoken in anger or in frustration. Lord, help me to use my tongue for the purpose for which You created it—to praise You and to encourage others. In the name of Jesus I pray. Amen.

⌒

To guard the presence and passion of God in your heart,
choose your words the way you choose your friends ... wisely.
Know they will be few but precious.
—Lisa Bevere

38

Live Like You Mean It

When a person initially becomes a Christian, an inside job happens that will cause that person to come alive in unseen ways. Sins are instantly and miraculously forgiven, which is an inner and eternal work. In the deepest parts of one's personhood, an intimate knowledge of God is now found and the desire is quietly birthed to please Him with all one's ways. The difference in one's soul is profound; there is fresh purpose, sweet revelation, and the certainty that you are loved completely by the One who created you. It's an inner work that has taken place for all of eternity.

And then comes the moment when the inner work must reveal itself in outer actions and words. This profound change is too great not to make a marked difference in the way that a person conducts himself or herself. This miraculous cleansing cannot just stay hidden but it must reveal itself for the world to see. The life and character of Christ, which is now in you, must come out of you. It's time to live like you mean it!

Put It Away

You will truly begin to live the life that God meant for you to live when you simply get rid of a few character traits that are holding you back from fullness, authenticity, and purpose. These attitudes and activities are never acceptable, they are never fulfilling and they are never Christlike.

Let all bitterness and wrath and anger and clamor and slander be put away from you, along with all malice. —Ephesians 4:31

I took the time to clean out my closet this month. I am almost embarrassed to admit that I probably had no less than twenty pairs of black pants in about four different sizes hanging out in the recesses of my overstuffed closet. I had sweaters that ranged in size from small to extra large, providing a panoramic view of my weight over the past ten years. I actually found a maternity top that I had worn for my last pregnancy, which was twenty-five years ago! And it's unbelievably awkward to admit that I discovered shirts with the tags still on them that were stuffed behind winter coats, rain jackets, and bathing suits.

So, I took a deep breath, bought a container of oversized black trash bags, and went to work. Please don't judge me ... but when I was finished, I had taken twelve huge bags of clothes to Goodwill—and I haven't missed any of those clothes! My closet is now clean, organized, and easy to straighten. I love my closet when I can manage it and when it doesn't manage me! I had to put outdated, ill-fitting, ridiculous clothes away. I did it and I am now free!

Outdated and Ill-Fitting

If we were best friends and you arrived at my home wearing an outfit that was inappropriate for the occasion or fit atrociously, I would gently offer you something else to wear. Because I try to be kind, I would try not to embarrass you, but my goal would be to love you enough to want you to look your very best! So consider me your best friend today as I help you with your emotional wardrobe. There are certain items that need to be replaced immediately! Will you let me help you with that?

Perhaps there are some outdated emotions in your emotional wardrobe that you need to toss. Maybe you have some imperfect attitudes and habits hanging in the closet of your heart that honestly don't look very good on you. You are going to love the wonderful freedom that you experience when you refuse to wear these emotional garments that are constricting and ill-fitting.

Cleaning out our emotional closets is not always easy, but Paul offers invaluable help and surprising expertise in this venture. He even has a list for you to consider in the cleaning process. According to Paul and the Holy Spirit, these are the things that you need to proactively search for and then dispose of completely and immediately. Now, as you read this list, examine your heart to see if you have been holding onto any of these ugly traits. Please don't just peruse the list quickly; read it prayerfully and ask the Holy Spirit to help you in your assessment. Remember, this is part of the discipline that it takes to live a vibrant life of incomparable joy!

+ Bitterness: an anger that refuses to offer forgiveness and only grows with time.

+ Wrath or rage: outbursts of anger for self-centered reasons. This includes becoming out of control because you feel that you lack control.

+ Anger: a simmering attitude of negativity and criticism that poisons every decision, every conversation, and every relationship.

+ Clamor: harsh, loud, angry words that erupt out of one's mouth with no regard for the damage that they will do.

+ Slander: defamation of character or gossip. Destructive and cruel, slander is usually based in pride.

+ Malice: a deliberate attempt to harm another person or ruin their reputation. It is birthed in evil and destroys relationships.

Could I challenge you to read through this ugly list one more time? As you read through it again, think of the most difficult person in your life and ask yourself if you have ever exhibited one of these character traits to that person. If you see your heart attitudes in this list, you must do something about it. First, ask the Lord to forgive you for treating someone in this manner, and then ask the person to forgive you. Perhaps you could even think of a way to bless the person beyond the forgiveness. What joy!

We are going to read the list one more time before we put it away; this time, it will be the most difficult read-through of all. As you read the list for the third time, ask yourself if you have ever treated someone whom you love dearly in this manner. If you have, the response is the same. Ask the Lord to forgive you and then go to the person and sincerely ask for forgiveness. What incomparable joy!

Would you pray with me today:

Lord Jesus, how I love serving You! How I treasure the lives of the people whom You have graciously given to me. Father, today, I need Your strength and Your power to rid my life of bitterness, wrath, anger, clamor, slander, and malice. Help me to be like You. In Jesus's name I pray. Amen.

⌒

A true disciple does not consider Christianity a part-time commitment. He has become a Christian in all parts of his life. He has reached the point where there is no turning back.
—A. W. Tozer

39

The Best for Last

I was raised in an extremely strict Christian home by an incredibly fun mother. Does that seem like a contradiction in terms to you? Mom made it easy for me to love the Lord and cope with the *thou shalt not's* in our home because she was always stirring up joy and celebration. In my young adult years, as we were discussing the way that she had raised me, she told me that whenever she had to say *no* to me as a child or as a teenager, she always tried to say a better *yes*.

"No, you can't go to that party," she would say as a grin captured her face, "but how would you like have some friends over here instead?"

"No, you can't wear that short skirt," she would quietly insist, "but I'd love to buy you something more appropriate."

"No, you can't listen to that music," she would coach me, "but I'd love to listen to some music together so we can find something to agree on and then I'll treat you to a new piano book."

I surmise that this is what Paul is doing in this final verse of Ephesians 4. He has told us that bitterness, wrath, anger, clamor, slander, and malice are not options for us—but he has a better yes!

Be kind to one another, tender-hearted, forgiving each other, just as God in Christ also has forgiven you.   —Ephesians 4:32

The Better Yes

I have a challenge for you today. Make a list of the qualities that you wish you had in a best friend. Would you want this friend to be a good listener? A servant? Have a good sense of humor? To be kind?

After you have made your list, then *you* become that person! You become the friend that you wish you had! Rather than waiting impatiently for some fantasy person to fulfill all of your needs, you have the power to become a purposeful and amazing friend!

If I were to make a list of the attributes that I deeply desired in a friend, I believe that Paul's list, found in Ephesians 4:32, would match my list. And so, today, I will become that person.

I will be kind to the people in my life. I will use kind words and exhibit kind actions. I will even begin to think kind thoughts about the people in my life. How amazing to understand that the Father is thinking kind thoughts about me all day long! I must begin to think like my Father thinks. Kindness always takes the initiative and so I will be assertively kind. I will be kind to the person who waits on me in the restaurant and I will be kind to my mother. I will speak words of kindness to my husband and I will show actions of kindness to my children. I will think kind thoughts about my neighbors and about my pastor. I say a resounding, "Yes!" to kindness.

I will become increasingly tenderhearted. I will not judge others or try to control their actions, but I will be compassionate toward them and endeavor to be sincerely sympathetic. I will not think that I always know best but I will listen with sensitivity and understanding. I am humbled by the Father's tender heart toward me and I will remind myself often that having and demonstrating a tender heart runs in the family. I will say a gentle yet firm, "Yes!" to having a tender heart.

I will constantly and generously forgive others. I will not hold onto hurts or petty grudges, but I will lavishly and generously allow the forgiveness of the Father to pour through me. I will remind myself often that it is more fun to forgive. I will confess forgiveness with my mouth even before I experience it in my heart. I will be the most extravagant forgiver of my entire generation! I will forgive much because I have been forgiven much by the One who loves me most and knows me best. I will say a humble yet powerful, "Yes!" to forgiveness.

Just Like Jesus

I truly feel sorry for people who don't know Jesus and yet continually try to live a life of joy and purpose. They are like a hamster on his little wheel, always working, always running, but always frustrated. There is no joy apart from Jesus and there is no purpose without His guidance and direction. Every area of our lives, like a sacred boomerang, should always return to becoming more and more like Jesus.

Paul ends his better *yes* with the words, *"just as God in Christ also has forgiven you"* (Ephesians 4:32).

Every character trait that we are called to embrace, every action of kindness or love, and each word of compassion or tenderness is a telling reflection of the Jesus in us. Think about it for a minute: you get to live life with the joy of Jesus! You get to activate the power of heavenly kindness in a human body. You are invited to live with the purpose of the gospel and demonstrate the character of God through every cell of your body! You are called to be a vibrant show-and-tell of what God is able to accomplish through one ordinary person. Now do it!

Would you pray this prayer with me today:

Jesus, I want more of You! Jesus, I want all of You! Fill me up until I nearly explode with Your goodness, Your love, Your patience, and Your joy! I accept the assignment that You have given to me, Father. I will be Your show-and-tell at this moment in history. In Jesus's matchless name I pray. Amen.

⌣⟩

The years of our pilgrimage are all too short to master it triumphantly. Yet this is what Christianity is for—
to teach men the art of life.
—Henry Drummond

Postscript

Dear Friend,

Well ... we did it, didn't we?

We have faithfully lingered over stunning verses in the New Testament that call us to a life of no regrets and heart-stirring vibrancy. How wonderful to know that this life of grand impact is not too hard to obtain, nor is it too difficult to understand.

We are His and He is ours. Such knowledge both overwhelms me and settles me!

It is His strength that empowers us.

It is His call that rouses us.

It is His pleasure that we seek.

The genuine call of God that echoes across the pages of Scripture is not a call to a certain place, nor is it the challenge to complete a specific accomplishment, but it *is* the call to everyday obedience.

It is the call to know Him!

It is the call to delight! We are absolutely delighted that we are unconditionally loved by God.

It is the call to persevere in spite of our own weaknesses.

I hope that you have discovered that in Scripture, we have all that we could ever need or ever desire to live a life of sterling joy.

Joy is not realized by accomplishing a lofty goal or by making all of our dreams come true.

Joy is discovered when I embrace Christ and all that He is.

Joy is delivered when I join my life with His in a stirring melody of worship.

Joy is the companion given on the journey when I follow His roadmap.

His purpose for each of our lives is to know Him and to be known by Him.

Scripture has enabled us, as mere human beings, to have a magnificent view of Him ... of His heart ... and of His plan for our lives.

Although you may never preach a sermon, let it be known that your life is a profound demonstration of the Father's character.

His mandate is clear: we are the pages upon which His character has been written.

You are our letter, written in our hearts, known and read by all men; being manifested that you are a letter of Christ, cared for by us, written not with ink but with the Spirit of the living God, not on tablets of stone but on tablets of human hearts.

—2 Corinthians 3:2–3

Do you understand now? You are the love letter that Christ has written to a world in pain! It is in you and through you that He will bring peace to confusion, kindness to enmity, and patience to discord.

It is in you and through you that Christ will love the world. And in this, you will discover a vibrant life of unquenchable joy and unmatched purpose.

Blessings and joy,

Carol

About the Author

The president and CEO of Carol McLeod Ministries, Carol McLeod is a popular speaker at women's conferences and retreats. She is the author of a dozen books, including *Significant: Becoming a Woman of Unique Purpose, True Identity, and Irrepressible Hope*; *StormProof: Weathering Life's Tough Times*; *Guide Your Mind, Guard Your Heart, Grace Your Tongue*; *Joy for All Seasons*; *Holy Estrogen*; and *Defiant Joy*.

Carol hosts a twice weekly podcast, *A Jolt of Joy!* on the Charisma Podcast Network, and a weekly podcast, *Significant*. Her weekly blog, *Joy for the Journey*, has been named in the Top 50 Faith Blogs for Women. Carol also writes a weekly column in *Ministry Today*.

She has written several devotionals for YouVersion, including "21 Days to Beat Depression," which has touched the lives of nearly one million people around the world. Her teaching DVD *The Rooms of a Woman's Heart* won the prestigious Telly Award for excellence in religious programming.

Carol was also the first women's chaplain at Oral Roberts University and served as chaplain on the university's Alumni Board of Directors for many years.

Carol has been married to her college sweetheart, Craig, for more than forty years and is the mother of five children in heaven and five children on earth. Carol and Craig also happily answer to "Marmee and Pa" for their captivating grandchildren.